RUNNING On EMPTY

AND LOOKING FOR THE NEAREST EXIT

ANNIE CHAPMAN

BETHANY HOUSE PUBLISHERS
Minneapolis, Minnesota 55438

P9-APL-650

Published by Bethany House Publishers
A Ministry of Bethany Fellowship, Inc.
11300 Hampshire Avenue South
Minneapolis, Minnesota 55438

Printed in the United States of America

Library of Congress Cataloging-in-Publication Data

Chapman, Annie.
  Running on empty and looking for the next exit : how smart women learn to cope with everyday life / Annie Chapman.
       p. cm.
  Includes bibliographical references.
  ISBN 1–55661–587–6
  1. Women—Psychology. 2. Housewives—Psychology.
3. Women—Religious life. 4. Housewives—Religious life.
5. Self-sacrifice. I. Title.
HQ1206.C449   1995
646.7'0082—dc20   95–39285
                                                            CIP

Dedicated to Alice Click,
a sweet sister and dear friend.
I am inspired by the quiet yet effective way
you speak out against injustice,
you care for the needy,
and you stand boldly for the yet-to-be-born.

Books by Annie Chapman

Running on Empty and Looking for the Nearest
   Exit!
Can I Control My Changing Emotions?
   (with Shaw & Littauer)

Books By Annie Chapman (with Maureen Rank)

Gifts Your Kids Can't Break
Married Lovers, Married Friends
Smart Women Keep It Simple

ANNIE CHAPMAN has been ministering to families with her husband, Steve, through their music and speaking for many years. They have several albums and books in national distribution, their music and message on the family have been featured in numerous magazines, and they perform nationwide in concerts every year. The Chapmans make their home in Nashville, Tennessee, with their children Nathan (18) and Heidi (15). They attend Christ Church in Nashville.

Contents

Introduction:
When the Fuel Gauge Is on "E" 9
1. Am I Having Fun Yet?............................. 11
2. If You Really Love Me, Then Help!.................. 21
3. How's the Weather in There? 33
4. I Know I Love My Family . . . I Just Can't
   Remember Why.................................. 51
5. What Price Success?.............................. 71
6. Stop the World: I Want to Get Off! 89
7. Me Forgive? Forget It! 107
8. Too Young to Die Old 123
9. Yes, Lord, But I Never Counted on This! 137
10. Can Worth Be Weighed on a Bathroom Scale?......... 151
11. Refueled and Refreshed 167

Introduction:

When the Fuel Gauge
Is on "E"

Two things drive me batty when I travel with my husband, Steve. (Which is nearly every week, since we've been ministering through music and seminars for the past twenty years.)

First of all, he enjoys driving the car with the fuel gauge pointing to empty. He protests, "There's so little adventure left in life. You have to grab it where possible." I think he needs to take up mountain climbing and leave me out of his need for adventure.

The second thing that makes me crazy is that he refuses to stop and ask directions when he's gotten us lost. Oh sure, he has another explanation. "With the high-tech approach to life these days," he says, "trying to find it on my own is the last frontier." Okay. So he's always gotten where we needed to go. And I've never had to lug a gas can. But he's given me enough fits and anxious moments that I'm entitled to complain!

As much as I hate to admit it, I'm a lot like Steve when it comes to traveling down life's highway. Sometimes I find myself without direction. Sometimes I refuse to stop and check my directions, even though I haven't felt like I've been in familiar territory for months. Too often I feel like I'm emotionally and spiritually on "E"—and I'm running on empty.

At this season in my life, I've had enough reckless adventure. I need peace of mind. I'm tired of pushing myself so hard, for so long, wondering if I'll make it to the next exit. I'm convinced that I need to learn how to find more strength and refreshment in an easier approach to life. As a wife and mother, as a woman who is active in the Christian community, I can't *stop* what I'm doing and just park. But I know it's time to wisely assess the direction my life is going and be honest about the resources I have—and those I need—so that I can fulfill the wonderful, surprising, challenging journey I call "my life." Will I really honor God with my life and respect the talents and dreams He's given me? Or will I fritter my days away on worry and busy-work, always helping other people on their journeys but wondering if I've even begun my own?

Considering the pace and demand of life today, it's no surprise that many of my family and friends face the same inner dilemmas. Because so many of them have expressed the same spiritual needs for new peace, less frenzy, and more meaningful contribution, their thoughts and experiences are reflected in these pages.

Facing the enormity of the task at hand as committed children of God, loving wives, busy mothers, devoted daughters, helpful friends, loyal employees, and concerned citizens, we women need the refreshing and refueling power of the work of Christ to help us reach our destination. Even though at times we may be *running on empty and looking for the nearest exit*, there is comfort in knowing that we need not run a solitary race.

1

Am I Having Fun Yet?

I admire people who know how to relax. When I drive by a house and see people lazily sitting on the porch, doing absolutely nothing, I envy their ability to just kick back. Steve and I made an attempt to relax one beautiful summer evening. Our idea was to take a leisurely stroll around the block, enjoy the sunset, and greet our neighbors. As we started to leave our yard, though, we began talking about the landscaping rocks we had placed alongside the driveway. We stood back and viewed them from every angle, then decided we weren't really pleased after all with how they looked. Before Steve could say, "You've got to be out of your mind!" I had coerced him into helping me manually remove those sixteen hundred pounds of river pebbles. Before it was over, we beamed the headlights of our car on us, determined to finish the job if it took all night.

Several times throughout that long night, I soaked in a tub of hot water, trying to soothe the muscle spasms in my arms. The next morning we left for a weekend of travel, singing, and ministry. We never got to that leisurely stroll.

For a long time, my family has expressed concern for me. They think I work too much and too hard. Not only do I drive myself, I drive others—and oddly enough I feel like *I'm* the one who's always being driven.

"Let's take a vacation day and go fishing," my family urged.

"You need it, Mom. You need to get away from everything and enjoy the great outdoors."

A perfect opportunity was coming up. The four of us were scheduled to sing in Alaska. So we made plans to stay over an extra day—for fun, rest, and adventure. Since I had never gone on any of the Famous Family Fishing Forays before, I resisted my regular tendency to be a stick-in-the-mud. I decided to trust my family to spirit me away in a small plane into the bush country of Alaska for a day of fishing. We were going to fish the King Salmon. It would be fun!

There is a basic reason I've never accompanied my family on fishing trips: I don't like to fish. I don't like the smell or the feel of fish. And unless they're heavily battered and deep-fried, I don't even like the *taste* of fish. And I'm not that crazy about the great outdoors, unless I'm poolside in a lounge chair with my tanning oils and a cold drink. Braving the elements and battling the wild did not sound that appealing, but being the dutiful mother, I cheerfully went along. So *I could relax.*

The morning started rather early with the buzz of the clock radio. Getting up at 5 A.M. so we could go relax seemed a bit strange, but who was I to complain? We gathered the gear, the ice cooler, and the waders. (Waders are hip boots you wear so you won't get wet while standing in the middle of a rushing river.) Soon our family sardine-squeezed into the little float-plane, along with three other men and their gear. I had no idea that public humiliation loomed just beyond that wild horizon of rugged mountains which I could begin to see now in the blue light of dawn.

The first glitch came when the pilot noticed the pontoons were sitting a bit low in the water. The total weight of the plane concerned him. He stuck his head into the passenger compartment and there—in front of everyone—asked us to tell our weight . . . *Out loud!* You must understand, I don't tell *anyone* what I weigh. My husband of over twenty years—the father of my children and my soulmate—doesn't even know what the scale and I know. I faked six years of continuous menstruation just so I could skip P.E. class in junior and senior high. I've avoided the doctor for the past four years because I don't want the nurse to weigh me. All my life I had succeeded in keeping the secret . . . *until that hideous moment.*

Everything seemed to shift into slow motion. The plane got

deathly silent, and all eyes turned accusingly on me, as if to say, "If you lie and this plane goes down, it will be all your fault." In my mind's eye I could see the headlines in the tabloids: WOMAN LIES ABOUT HER WEIGHT KILLING ENTIRE FAMILY. Life and death had me by the throat. I took a deep breath, and before God and the angels I said, "_____." (Are you kidding? Did you really think I'd tell you, too?)

Everyone seemed unusually quiet. I was sure someone was thinking, *Lady, that's what my car weighs.* . . .

Heidi, our daughter, was stunned. In an ominous whisper, she said, "You told your weight?!" I gave no reply. I was already tired and miserable.

As I stared out the window moments later, deafened by the propellers' roar, I suspected my chances of feeling refreshed and relaxed were slim. And that was the only thing that was slim that day.

It got worse when we pontooned to a landing on a wilderness lake and I realized the pilot was *leaving* us in the bush country. Oh sure, he *said* he'd return that evening at six o'clock. But did anyone really know this man? All that was left for me was to resign myself to enjoy fishing . . . for the next *ten* hours!

We made our way to the site where the fish were supposed to be. It was quite exhilarating: the breathtaking scenery, the bitter cold wind, and the bloodsucking mosquitos. Since I had never fished, I was instructed in how to cast the line into the water and found, to my amazement, that it wasn't so bad after all. *Look what I've missed out on all my life,* I thought.

Heidi is quite an enthusiastic fisherman. It's fun to see her standing beside her dad, fishing with true enjoyment. About forty-five minutes into that morning's sport, Heidi decided to move off the sandbar where we were fishing and go to the other side. When she changed positions, she accidentally stepped off the sandbar and up to her waist in water, well over her waders. She was soaked. The air was around fifty degrees, and the water was *much* colder.

Here we were, stranded in the middle of nowhere, and I had not thought to bring a stitch of extra clothing. No towels or blankets. We fished Heidi from the river, and fortunately, one of the men who was fishing alongside us let Heidi change into the extra clothes he'd brought. We made a fire and warmed Heidi up, and soon the problem was solved so everyone could get back to fishing . . . everyone, that is, except me. As the family enjoyed an invigorating morning on the river, the "eternal mother" stood on the shore like a human clothesline, continuously turning Heidi's clothes, drying them by the fire. Wasn't this fun?

Every once in a while someone would call back to me from their fishing spot and ask, "How's it going? Are you all right?" Heidi yelled over, "Don't burn my jeans, Mom! Those are my favorites."

Yes, my family was right. I needed a day away from the mundane routine of everyday chores—you know, like doing laundry. Standing there on the shore trying to keep from singeing Heidi's jeans and unsuccessfully keeping smoke out of my eyes, I gained a newfound appreciation for my life. There was even a special spot of affection for my electric clothes dryer.

With Heidi's clothes finally dried, I returned to the river—smelling like a hot dog. The rest of the day was great fun and very relaxing. I definitely want to go fishing again . . . someday . . . maybe . . . (if my family grovels). . . .

Why, I wonder, do I let Life's Great Speeding Bus tailgate me from behind, pushing me further and further over the speed limit?

I'll be the first to admit that *I am a driven person*. It's not that I think I can "do it all," but just doing it at all takes everything I've got . . . plus some.

Standing on that riverbank opened my eyes a bit that day. I began to realize that I'm the one who always jumps in to help, even when I've been coerced into doing something that wasn't my idea in the first place. I'm a can-do person and everyone knows it. Especially my family. So they let me do for them what I've done graciously and without complaint all their lives. And I feel tired. And a bit resentful. But the more tired I get, the more determined I am to grit my teeth and keep going.

For the first time in my life—in the overwhelming grandeur of the Alaskan wilderness—I awakened to the fact that I didn't want to be the Can-Do Lady anymore. I realized I needed to give myself permission and time to find out what refreshes me. How could I distribute the weight of life's responsibilities so it didn't land on my shoulders quite so often? How could I find a balance between *activities that build me up and give me joy in accomplishment* and *activities that grind me down*?

Perfect Has Its Price

Trying to live the image of The Woman Who Has It All Together can be quite costly. It can take its toll in many ways. It can even cost a friendship.

After Heidi was born, my best friend did not once bring me a meal or offer to help me with Nathan, who was three. Even though I'd helped her many times, she didn't do anything that I expected her, as my dearest friend, to do. For a while I harbored hurt feelings. Our friendship cooled. One day she asked what was wrong, and I told her how disappointed and hurt I felt that she didn't help me when it was so obvious I needed her.

She looked stunned. "I didn't think you *needed* anyone! You seemed to have it all together."

It was true that I gave birth to my daughter without any medication, and within the hour of her delivery, got out of bed and walked down to check on her in the nursery. I came home within thirty-six hours after her birth and then fixed a huge dinner for all the family who came to see the baby that same day. Never once in the days that followed did I take a nap. (What could *possibly* have given my friend the idea that I was self-sufficient and didn't need any help?)

If I'd let the truth be known, I was dying inside. Of course I needed help, but there was something driving me on. I wanted and needed the help, but I just couldn't bring myself to ask for it.

I, like so many women, have lived my life with the notion that asking for help is a sign of weakness. I'll accept help if offered, but I won't beg. Even to this day, if I ask Steve to take out the garbage and he doesn't do it right away, then I'll go ahead and do it. I don't get mad, and he doesn't take offense. We both understand that I don't ask twice.

There's work enough for us to simply keep the basics done— food on the table, clothes to wear, and a path carved out so we can walk through the house. Add to this heavy work load an outside job, children, plus a perfectionist attitude, and you have the makings for at best, exhaustion, and at worst, a complete collapse.

What's at the Bottom of the Self-Reliance Pit?

Why do we drive ourselves into the ground with work and overactivity? Could it be that we have somehow connected our worth with our work? Coming from a large family and being raised on a dairy farm, I see how that can easily happen. The economic success of the family was determined by the willingness of the children to work and help with the chores. In an agricultural setting, children are generally not a financial drain but an asset to the economy of the family. This is not a bad thing. As a child, I was proud that I could milk the cows, feed the pigs, and basically help lighten the load for my parents.

However, with the great emphasis on doing a job, there is a tendency to confuse one's worth with one's work. This insanity shows up when I do crazy things like cooking a meal for family and friends when we brought Heidi home from the hospital. I should have rested and let someone else cook the meal.

There are women reading these pages who can't bear to sit down and let someone else do a job they consider their responsibility. When I suggested that someone else should cook the meal, my fellow "perfectionists" started thinking, "What if no one else was willing to do it?"

It's simple. If no one else cooked the meal, then the people would have to eat somewhere else. In this day and age, there are restaurants and grocery stores. No one need go hungry. There comes a time when we must admit that we are not to carry the full responsibility for everything and everyone. In the midst of our complaining about no one helping us, we have to come to grips with the fact that if we do it all ourselves, then no one needs to help us. We have chosen our own poison, and the misery we feel is at our own hand. Somehow, perfectionists seem to believe that the world will stop revolving if they stop moving.

My sister Gayle, who has five children (three were added to the family in a twelve-month period through adoption), admits there was a time when she had only two children that she not only thought she *should* do it all, but she *could* do it all. However, with the added work of three more children and the additional stress of incorporating the adopted children into an already established family system, she no longer could pull it off. Now she has to enlist the help of her children, her husband, and even her friends. The children have household chores of dusting, vacuuming, and cleaning bathrooms. Her perfectionist tendencies have to be altered in order to accept jobs that do not meet her high standards of cleanliness. However, she has learned to live with the margin of error. Gayle's need for help, she now sees, is a blessing to her entire family. The work gets done, the children are helping the family, and most important, they are learning responsibility.

The Freedom Found in Having Nothing to Prove

Sometimes, only the passage of time can help us overcome the overwhelming need to appear totally in control. Whether we find ourselves overworking, overspending, overparenting— whatever we choose as our obsession—there is a valuable freedom found when we can accept that our worth is not based on what we do, how we do it, or what others think of us.

I noticed at my ten-year high school reunion that nothing had really changed that much. The ones who were on top in school were still striving to give the appearance of "top dog." The little guys either didn't show up or hung out with the friends who had shared the lower rungs on the popularity ladder of high school. The differing groups mostly kept to their designated slots from the years past. Personally, I was rather disappointed. I had hoped that ten years would have evened things out a bit. But to all appearances it had not.

When I went back for my twenty-year reunion, things had changed. Somehow, gravity knows no social status. The cute little cheerleaders shared the battle of the bulge, even as the famed football team sported balding heads and spare tires. There was something rather refreshing in knowing that even those who still looked young and perfect were the same age as those who looked like a horse that had been "rode hard and put up wet." It was a much more relaxed atmosphere the second time around.

Now it's nearly time to go back for my thirty-year reunion. I imagine there are a few women who have started their midlife diets, and some men who have their new hairpiece on order, but for the majority, enough time and maturity have transpired to set most of us at ease about ourselves.

For me, my goal has become to learn a little more each day that I no longer have to prove my worth by my particular obsession—my doing. It's fine to work hard, but my job does not define who I am. I am more than my work. Regardless of what my cultural experiences have taught me, my worth is ultimately connected to the fact that even while I was a sinner, Christ died for me. If my Creator deems me worthy of His love and His Son, then I am indeed worthy. God loves me even when I'm lying on the couch doing nothing. For some, this is no great revelation, but for those of us who are in a constant "do" mode, learning that resting is a good exercise is a valuable lesson.

My worth—or *who* I am—has nothing to do with whether the blades on the fan are dusty or clean. I want to learn that there are responsibilities I must fulfill, but some of that work others can do. I do not have to do it all. If it doesn't get done today, I mustn't despair: it will be there tomorrow.

Taking on Realistic Responsibilities

So what are some of the things we must do to fight this tendency to do too much?

We must be willing to admit that we need help. This may seem a simple thing to do, that is, unless you are afflicted with the deadly syndrome called, "If you want it done right, then do it yourself." I knew a pastor who had never learned the art of delegating authority. He did it all from a fear that nothing would be done right. From cleaning the pews to teaching Sunday school to those who sat in the pews, he did everything. Consequently, no one ever learned to fill the void when he died from a stress-induced heart attack. The basic hindrance to asking for help is pride. Pride goes before destruction, and it will destroy those of us who refuse to reach out for help.

We must evaluate what it is that keeps us from reaching out for help. Is it an unwillingness to accept less than perfect results? Would you rather make your child's bed than have the bedspread on cockeyed? This is something you have to decide. If you refuse the help of those around you because they may not do it well enough, then you are not allowing them to learn to do the job better. For a while, make the bed together. Then have your child stand back and take a look at it. If the bedspread is crooked, let your child correct it. Your family will never learn to do things right unless they are given the chance.

Do you refuse help because you nurture a martyr complex? Do you enjoy complaining that you are the only one who does anything around the house? Sometimes our complaining is just another way of getting attention. Some people believe that negative attention is better than no attention at all. If you are feeling neglected and unappreciated, talking about these feelings is much more productive than creating a crisis of attention.

We must determine why we overcommit ourselves to activities and obligations. Is it because this is where we get our personal "perks"?

Think about your own situation. You may give an overabundance of time and attention to the benevolent work at the church because the people you help show more appreciation to you than those at your own house. This may also be the reason your husband is so willing to repair the neighbors' plugged-up sink and leave you wading in ankle-deep water. If the neighbor lady appreciates your husband's kindness and willingness to help, and she expresses it, while you're busy complaining that he didn't fix your sink earlier, that's dangerous. We must realize that we often do that which feeds our hunger for attention or satisfies our unmet needs.

But let's not be discouraged. There *is* hope for us "runaway" doers! In the pages that follow we'll look at some practical ways to lighten the burdens of responsibility that are depleting our energies. Together we'll discover where to find help and how to enlist it. We'll look at the direction we're traveling to see if it's really where we want to go; and then we'll examine various obstacles and roadblocks as well as opportunities for changing our course. Finally, we'll explore ways to incorporate the Lord's strength and purpose into our lives for refueling and refreshment for the journey ahead. Come ride with me!

2

If You Really Love Me, Then Help!

I'm not saying that being a mother can cause brain damage, but I will admit I've not had a complete thought in over eighteen years. Not long ago I was talking to a friend who related a conversation with a frazzled mother of two. The mother was asked to tell about her children. In a weary, out-of-breath tone she simply responded, "I have two children, ages six and four, a boy and a girl."

My friend continued the conversation by asking, "Well, who's the oldest?"

The woman, taxed with responding to yet another inquiry, answered, "The six-year-old."

There are women who desperately see the need to be organized, and yet they have a major problem: they have to be able to think in order to organize. Thinking can be quite a challenge if your brains have been siphoned by your own children.

In my previous book, *Smart Women Keep It Simple*, I talked about the virtuous woman in Proverbs 31.[1] I get the feeling that somehow she was able to hold it all together. Not only does it

---

[1] Annie Chapman and Maureen Rank, "Why I Hate the Proverbs 31 Woman," *Smart Women Keep It Simple* (Minneapolis, Minn.: Bethany House Publishers, 1992).

seem that her brain was still intact, but it was functioning quite impressively. Here, our example of the perfect, godly woman was doing it all. I get tired just thinking about her many exploits. She made her own clothes, got up early, went to bed late, always had dinner on time, cultivated a garden, bought and sold property, and took care of the poor and needy. In her spare time she was a loving, supportive wife who was beautiful, fit, and accomplished. Whew! Give me a break.

How did she do it all? Is this the standard God requires of me? Am I justified in living my sometimes insane lifestyle that often leaves my tank empty along life's road?

In my crying out to God for wisdom and His plan for me, I have concluded that comparing my life to the woman in Proverbs 31 is not quite fair. At that time a wealthy woman would have had many servants to help, and the activities listed occurred during a lifetime, not all in one day. It would be unwise, for instance, for a modern mother of small children, who typically has no help with childcare or housework, to feel guilty because she is not able to teach a Sunday school class or help in the nursery at church. She shouldn't try to do more than is humanly possible simply because others expect it of her.

Life Is a Matter of Choices, Limitations, and Adjustments

There is help for the frazzled woman. For those who can afford it, an outside cleaning service can be an alternative to having a nervous breakdown. What a glorious life you could have if you knew that every Monday morning a crew would arrive with a truckload of helping hands and cleaning gear! You could leave the house and come back three hours later with everything restored to its original *Mop and Glo* shine and *Good Housekeeping* standard of excellence. Help with cooking, cleaning, and laundry is available for the right price. However, to many of us, the cost would look like a government loan. The possibility of hiring another set of hands is not always a practical solution.

Because of limitations—like economic restraints—another choice must be considered. If not the "Handy-Dandy Cleaning Crew" listed in the yellow pages, then to whom can the weary, cost-conscious woman turn for help? The choice is obvious, but because radical attitude adjustments must be made, it is easy to resist this alternative. Her help is found in those who are called FAMILY AND FRIENDS.

Now I know what you're about to say. You *have* been asking for help—*begging* even—but your cries seem to fall on deaf ears. Perhaps your family doesn't know how serious you are. Believe me, you are not alone! I heard recently of a mother whose family refused to help out with the housework, even though she was holding down a full-time job outside of the home. After coming home night after night to find the house a mess and begging for help with no response, she finally "snapped" and hammered a big sign in the front yard for all to see: "Mother on Strike." Did her family get the message? You'd better believe it! Especially when the TV camera crews showed up. The father and children wound up admitting on national television that they'd been unfair to expect so much of their wife and mother, and they had all sat down together to negotiate a settlement. They even drew up written contracts to agree on specific terms. They had to admit that life was better now: Their home no longer resembled a pigpen, and their mom wasn't so stressed out all the time.

You may not want to call public attention to yourself as this mother did, but you do need to find a way to let your family know that "Supermom" has resigned and it's time for them to pick up the slack. It could be that your family simply doesn't know *how* to help you. You may need to show them.

Proverbs 22:6 tells us that we should "train up a child in the way he should go." That training involves a lot of things—including teaching your children good attitudes about work. The temptation is always great—especially if you're a perfectionist—simply to do the job yourself and do it "right." But then your children miss out on valuable instruction.

The following are some suggestions on *how* we can train our families to help carry the weight of responsibility.

Never Too Young to Help!

In her book *The Fifteen-Minute Organizer*, Emilie Barnes shares some wonderful ideas on how to reach out to our children for help. As a woman who at one time was the mother of five children under five, she is definitely qualified to speak on the subject.

Here are some practical ideas she gives on organizing the children to help around the house.

1. Give clearly defined directions.
2. Keep the jobs realistic.
3. Avoid criticism.
4. Above all, praise, praise, praise.

Barnes suggests that we write the jobs down on individual pieces of paper and put them in a basket. Then allow each child to choose two or three jobs from the basket each week.

For my own family I've adapted this idea by listing all the jobs that need to be done—along with a deadline for completion—on 3 × 5 cards. The kids are then given the responsibility of completing each job before the deadline. Because my children are older, they respond well to this approach. Somehow, reading the job themselves rather than my telling them seems to defuse the irritation factor of being "told" what to do. An added benefit is that the children have some freedom to choose how to arrange their work time, giving them valuable experience in decision making.

But beware! The children *will* compare cards to see if they are being treated fairly. For example, two of Nathan's routine jobs are mowing the grass and weed-eating, while Heidi does the ironing and laundry. They have decided that these are comparable jobs and that this is a fair division of work.

For younger children, Barnes suggests making a chart with each job listed on it. As the job is completed the child receives a sticker or star. By the end of the week, if all jobs have stickers indicating satisfactory completion, then it's reward time. Rewards can vary according to desirability—anything from money to a trip to McDonald's. And remember, there is nothing that can replace *praise* for a child's efforts and accomplishments.

In addition, Barnes says, "If you want your children to grow up believing that the mess belongs to the person who made it, don't teach them they are 'helping Mommy.' Instead, applaud them for making *their* bed, dressing *themselves*, and putting away *their* toys . . . having the mind-set that the child's room belongs to the child."[2]

---

[2]Emilie Barnes, *The Fifteen-Minute Organizer* (Eugene, Ore.: Harvest House Publishers, 1991), p. 76.

For me this was the most sensible statement in the entire book—a simple truth I overlooked for all of my twenty-something years of family life!

Here are some more helpful hints Ms. Barnes suggests for teaching children.

1. Provide low shelves on which to put toys, books, sweaters, and jackets. A floor-to-ceiling wooden pole can provide storage space for stuffed animals. Screw cup hooks into the pole and sew curtain rings onto each stuffed animal so the child can arrange them on the pole. Your child can even help with the sewing.

2. Make paper placemats and draw the shapes of the fork, spoon, plate, and glass on them. This way even your preschool children can learn the proper placement of the eating utensils without your having to stand over them.

3. Give each child a pillowcase, or trashbag, and send them to pick up toys, trash, and paper. Remember to praise them for their work.

4. When you teach children to dress themselves, keep in mind their limitations. Evaluate carefully as you buy their clothes, choosing comfortable, coordinating outfits where any combination matches. Keep pants in a bottom drawer and tops in the drawer above it. Let your children have fun "mixing and matching" their outfits.

5. Above all, make chores fun! Don't bark out orders. Be creative. When you keep a fun attitude, the children will also. And they'll grow up with a positive view of work.

The time it takes to teach our children to do simple jobs will be more than made up as we gain some relief from the work, and even more important, it will provide our children with valuable life skills.

This poem by Joy Allison is one my mother read to me throughout my childhood.

"I love you, Mother," said little John;
Then forgetting his work, his cap went on,
And he was off to the garden swing,
And she had the wood and the water to bring.

"I love you, Mother," said rosy Nell;
"I love you more than tongue can tell."

Then she teased and pouted half the day,
Till her mother was glad when she went to play.

"I love you, Mother," said little Nan;
"Today I'll help you all I can;
"My doll and playthings I know will keep!"
Then she rocked the baby fast asleep.

Stepping softly, she brought the broom,
And swept the floor and tidied the room.
Busy and happy all day was she,
Helpful and good as a child could be.

"I love you, Mother," again they said,
Three little children going to bed.
How do you think the mother guessed,
Which of them really loved her best?

"Help me, Honey!"

With many of us working so hard at trying to "do it all," it is not surprising that we find ourselves constantly running with the fuel gauge on empty, our energies seriously depleted. This deeply affects all of our relationships. For those of us who are married, it is indeed a challenge to keep the love fires burning when we ourselves are nearly burnt out.

I spoke recently with a panel of busy wives and asked them what things their husbands could do to lighten their loads. Their responses were not filled with the expected suggestions of, "I wish he'd do the dishes," or, "He should pick up after himself." I was surprised to find their list to be even more basic. Their comments (below) may help you put some of your own needs into words. A first step in being able to ask others for help is admitting you have needs and identifying what those needs are.

It's not always easy to ask your husband for help—especially when you know how busy *he* is—but try to find some quiet time alone to bring up the subject and show him this list of ideas. It could help break the ice and get you started on some serious dialogue together about how best to overcome the pressures of daily living that are threatening to "run you off the road." It is certainly in his best interests for you to tell him how you feel and to let him be that loving support you need.

If you really love me, then . . .

1. *Surprise me.* Take me out on a date without my having to ask. And, if you really want me to feel special, then arrange for the sitter, too.

When I'm having an especially difficult day, bring home a pizza, or make the offer to go out to eat. Even if I don't take you up on the offer, it makes me feel loved that you even suggested it.

I want to be more to you than just our children's mother. I want to be your wife and lover.

Help me have fun again. I get so tired of changing dirty diapers and wiping up spilled milk. Sometimes I think I've forgotten how to laugh. So much of my life is barking out orders and correcting behavior. I really need to lighten up. Help me laugh again—by having fun with me.

2. *Value my work.* I don't expect you to do *all* the housework, but when you leave messes around, expecting me to clean them up, I feel like a slave. If you value my work, then our children will also reflect this attitude.

I would never go into your office and hit the "delete" button on your computer at the end of the day, wiping out all of the work you've done. But that's how I feel when the work I've done with the house is so quickly "deleted."

I need you to thank me for dinner. There is a time for discussing fat content, or the selection of menu, but not at the end of a tiring day. Sometimes I'm very vulnerable and cannot handle criticism. With so much of my work undone so quickly, all I have left at the end of the day to show what I've done is your "thank-you." And I need to hear it. You work very hard, and I know that. I work hard too, and I need to know you appreciate it.

3. *Let me be me.* When you unknowingly compare me with your mother, or the pastor's wife, or the lady down the street, I feel worthless. I need you to look at my strengths, rather than my weaknesses. I already know there are plenty of weaknesses to see, but I feel more worthwhile when you recognize my positive characteristics.

I need you to help me feel desirable. Don't tease me about my appearance or physical flaws. Don't criticize me in front of others, even in a joking way. If I think you're unhappy with my appearance, it's very difficult for me to love you physically the way I want to, and the way *you* need to be loved. When you hold me, I need you to tell me that you find me appealing, lovely, even beautiful. If you believe me to be pretty, I will be. You're the only one I need and want to please, and only you can chase the "ugly duckling" in me away so the lovely swan can be yours.

All it takes is a word or a look of disapproval from you, and I start to doubt my decisions or actions. When you manipulate me with guilt, you crush the real person inside me. I need your support, not your control.

4. *Leave me alone.* I don't mean I want to be alone all the time, but there are times when I need you to take the children out to dinner and let me stay home. A cup of chicken soup in the quietness of solitude can be more delicious than a filet mignon in a noisy restaurant. Quiet is something I need but rarely experience.

Leave me alone so I can think a complete thought, or read a book. I used to be creative, and I still need to be from time to time. Spend time with the children and let me take an uninterrupted bath. Put the children to bed without coming and asking me, "Where are the children's toothbrushes?"

5. *Pray for me.* I need you to encourage me spiritually. There are times when I want to run away. With all the pressures you deal with, I'm sure you have those times too, but I've found that if I can "run to the Lord," I can find the strength I need to go on. Ecclesiastes 4:6 says, "One hand full of rest is better than two fists full of labor and striving after wind."

Jesus knew the need to get away from the daily grind, and when you pray for me, I make wiser decisions on how to draw from His stamina.

"I've fallen, and I don't want to get up!"

Naomi had experienced the deep sorrows of life. Forced from her beloved homeland of Bethlehem in order to escape starvation, she and her husband, Elimelich, moved to pagan Moab. While in Moab Elimelich died, leaving Naomi with her two sons.

Her sons married Moabite women. A few years later her sons both died, leaving her alone with her daughters-in-law. When the famine in Bethlehem ended, Naomi decided to return to her homeland. Knowing the difficulty of adjusting to a foreign land,

Naomi released her daughters-in-law back to their own families. "Go home," Naomi said. "Go back to your mother. There's nothing for you with me."

The daughters-in-law protested and affirmed their love for her, but Naomi insisted. Orpha kissed her and left, but Ruth chose to go with her mother-in-law. Perhaps Ruth saw Naomi's need of her. Or, perhaps it was her commitment and love for her deceased husband that compelled her to refuse Naomi's command to leave. Even more plausible, Ruth probably desired to go with Naomi to be where Jehovah God was worshiped. Ruth's converted heart longed to leave the ways of her people, with their idol worship of Baal, and cleave to Naomi's God. Naomi needed Ruth, and Ruth needed Naomi.

When they returned to Bethlehem, Naomi made no pretense of her state of mind. "Do not call me Naomi (which means 'pleasant'); but call me Mara (which means 'bitter'), for the Almighty has dealt very bitterly with me. I went out full, but the Lord has brought me back empty" (Ruth 1:20–21a).

Naomi had fallen, and she didn't want to get up. However, Ruth was her friend. She looked beyond Naomi's negativity and sought to lift her up. And God honored Ruth's commitment to Naomi by blessing her with a godly husband and son, making her the great-grandmother of David, Israel's greatest king. Among her descendants was the Messiah himself.

Don't we all need a "Ruth" in our lives? A friend who will stick by us and help us when we're down. A friend who can help us be a "Naomi" rather than a "Mara." A true friend "who multiplies joys and divides grief."

We all need to find such a friend, a friend in whom we can confide and from whom we feel free to ask for help. Our children and our spouse can only do so much. In order to have such a friend, we also need to *be* a friend—one who is willing to help another sister in need. It goes both ways.

Listen to some ideas the panel of women suggested when asked to finish this sentence: *If you're really my friend, then . . .*

1. *Go to lunch with me.* I know you're busy, but take some time to cultivate our friendship.
2. *Listen to me talk without judgment or criticism.* If I'm asking your advice, then be honest with me and tell me the truth.
3. *Keep my confidences.* When I tell you something, don't tell

anyone else. I need to be able to trust you.

4. *Pray for me.* Sometimes I have hurts no one can heal but God. It's a tremendous blessing to know that you are praying for me. It makes hearing God's voice a little clearer.

5. *Help me.* When you know I've had a tough time, then bring me a casserole. Come take my child for the day. Swap errands with me. Bring me a gallon of milk. Send me a card of encouragement.

Don't *let* me say no. When you ask me if I need help, don't take no for an answer. Know me well enough to see that I don't readily accept help, even when I need it. But, on the other hand, don't *make* me say yes. When you want me to do something, and I would like to but can't, please don't press me until I agree. For example, you may want me to go to a movie with you, when I really want and need some quiet time with my husband.

6. *Let me help you.* Tell me how I can help, and then let me. I need to think about someone else besides myself. So don't rob me of the blessing of helping you.

The following poem by Roy Croft has been a favorite of mine for many years. The true essence of friendship is expressed in these lines.

> I love you not only for what you are,
>   but for what I am when I am with you;
> I love you not only for what you have made of yourself,
>   but for what you are making of me;
> I love you not for closing your ears to the discords in me,
>   but for adding to the music in me by worshipful listening;
> You have done it without a touch, without a word,
>   without a sign.
> You have done it just by being yourself.
> Perhaps that is what being a friend means, after all.

What is the answer for those of us who are bone-tired and weary of life? Continuing down the path of self-sufficiency is not a virtue. We are not *weak* when we ask for help. We are *wise*. The words spoken to us through the prophet Isaiah give us the answer and the direction we need to be the kind of godly woman we want to be. Let the words of Isaiah 40:28–31 feed your soul: "Don't you yet understand? Don't you know by now that the everlasting God, the Creator of the farthest parts of the earth, never grows faint or weary? No one can fathom the depths of his understanding. He gives power to the tired and worn out, and strength to the weak. Even the youths shall be exhausted, and the young men [and women] will all give up. *But they that wait upon the Lord shall renew their strength. They shall mount up with wings like eagles; they shall run and not be weary; they shall walk and not faint"* (TLB, emphasis added).

Teach us, Lord, to wait. Amen.

3

How's the
Weather in There?

We got home on a Monday, after a long, arduous four days of traveling and singing from one city to another. A dull headache had plagued me the entire trip. Knowing I was leaving again in four days wasn't helping either. Needing to be in the office on Tuesday, I was left with a mere few hours to get the clothes unpacked and to the cleaners, and to get the house reconstructed after the weekend and made ready for company coming on Wednesday. I had more work to do than was humanly possible, given the best state of mind.

In desperation, I did two irrational things. First, I went to the local farmers market and bought flowers and shrubs to plant. As I drove up to the house with the back of our car loaded down with peat moss and plants, I felt rather foolish. I knew I was crazy for taking on such a frivolous project when there was so much work to do, but I was overwhelmed and was not thinking logically. I told myself, "I always do everything everyone else expects of me—why can't I do something I *want* to do?" So I planted flowers.

The second thing I did (after I planted the flowers) was equally irrational: I ran away from home. Actually, I went to my sister Becky's house and didn't leave word with Steve as to where I was. I knew he would be worried about me, but at that moment I didn't care. I was on the verge of collapse and needed a change of surroundings—someplace safe and peaceful. So I went to my sister's house. This proved the extent of my irrational state of mind: She has four preschoolers!

Becky laughed when I told her I had run away from home and when I asked if she would put me up. Somehow she couldn't picture anyone wanting to run to *her* situation. I sat on the floor and played with her children for a couple of hours. She made me a cup of tea and we talked.

After a while I actually started to feel better and reluctantly made my way back home. As I came closer to my house, I started to feel a bit guilty about the stress Steve must be feeling not knowing my whereabouts. When I drove up and looked around, I saw that no one was home. Part of me felt a smug sense of satisfaction. Steve must be out combing the streets, calling my name, pleading with the Lord for my safety and soon return. Maybe it would be good for him to feel a little panicked, since I myself was living on the verge of a panic attack most of the time.

The time alone helped me pull myself together. I unpacked a few things, threw some clothes in the washer, and put a chicken in the oven for dinner.

Steve finally got home. I quietly continued my work in the kitchen. Any second he'd rush in, fall at my feet, and *beg* me never to do that to him again. Braced to console his wounded spirit, I stood ready as he walked into the kitchen.

"So, what have you been doing today?" he inquired cheerfully, rummaging in the refrigerator. "I played golf this afternoon with a friend. I just needed to get out of the house." He found a can of cola, popped the top, and swigged. "You know, Annie, you should get out more yourself."

He grabbed a fistful of grapes from the fruit bowl and walked out—leaving me stewing at the stove. He didn't even know I'd been gone! How depressing—to run away from home, and have no one know it.

On that particular occasion I really wanted Steve to *notice* how badly I needed a break. I wanted him to "fix" my feelings of desperation and do for me what I had for so long refused to do for myself. But how could I expect him to notice my true feelings when I had done such an expert job of hiding them from him?

No one else can really take responsibility for the "weather" inside of us. A sunny disposition—or a cloudy, gloomy one—is not the result of what others do or don't do for us. *We* are the ones who choose which attitudes are going to control us. And when we find ourselves struggling with depressing or despairing thoughts, that should be a signal that we need to take responsibility for what's going on inside of us. It's time for us to take stock and notice what needs we have that are not being met.

If we don't take time to notice our own need—if we don't think we're important enough to pay attention to—why would anyone else?

So what can you do when you need to get off the speeding highway of your life? Is it possible to manage the excess stress when you're fixing to blow a gasket?

Let's look at a few simple stress-management techniques that provide a good starting place to help take the panic out of pressure.

Brightening Your Mood

We've heard a lot about being happy in recent years. In the past if people had something to eat, some clothes to wear, and a place to sleep they considered themselves as doing all right. These days if you don't have the necessities, plus a bunch of the added extras, then you are somehow being denied your rights as an American citizen. Did you know that 98 percent of all Americans own televisions, and 77 percent own VCR's? Even the poorest of Americans, by the world's standards, would be considered wealthy. The average income for an American family is $40,000. Compare that to the country of Haiti, with a yearly income of $240.

Possessing "stuff," being "somebody," and going "somewhere" are all considered essential components of being content, happy, and achieving success in today's society. Even though the average American possesses much materially, when overwhelmed by the demands of life, it is still easy for many to slip into the doldrums.

How do we move beyond our own troubles and maintain a positive attitude? An important step in the right direction is to surround ourselves with positive people. That's one of the best "mood brighteners" I know.

A Good Friend Is Like a Glass of Cool Water on a Hot Day

Most people will admit they harbor some negative attitudes toward their in-laws. But I can honestly say that two of the most positive people in my life are my in-laws P.J. and Lillian Chapman. When they come to visit our family, they know they are stepping into suburbia's rendition of Grand Central Station. You can get dizzy just sitting and watching everyone going in a million different directions. P.J. and Lillian adjust to the situation very quickly. Instead of being "company" that demand attention and being entertained, they become another pair of helpful hands. Lillian always helps in a spirit of humility and service. I never feel her help is an indictment of my inability to do it all; rather, she helps me do things I otherwise would not be able to get done. For example, the last time they visited, Lillian cleaned out all my kitchen cabinets and put down new shelf paper—one of those "I'll-get-to-it-someday" jobs. What a joy to open up the doors and see clean, organized cabinets!

Meanwhile, P.J. painted the interior of our entire house. We hadn't painted anything since we had moved in six years earlier, and as it stood, Steve wasn't going to get to it for another six years. At least. The hallmark of my in-laws is *they always leave our home and our lives better than they found them.* This is the best definition I know for "positive people."

Another time—when I was seriously "losing it"—my sister Becky refreshed me. She offered me an appreciative balance of sympathy for my situation, but also an admonishment to pull it together. She urged me to slow down after telling me the story about a well-known Christian woman who "burned the candle" at both ends and eventually burned out personally and professionally. I needed my sister to be my friend, and she was. She refreshed me by being there, listening to my list of woes, expressing a caring attitude, and encouraging me to practice what I preach: to depend on the Lord as my source of strength and help in times of trouble. She instructed me according to Psalm 27:13–14: "I would have *despaired* unless I had believed that I would see the goodness of the Lord in the land of the living. Wait for the Lord; be strong, and let your heart take courage; yes, wait for the Lord." Because of her friendship, my sister helped restore a bright mood in me.

Positive people can be a real boost, but beware—they can also create unspoken standards that are impossible to live up to. Instead of helping us to feel better, they can make us feel inferior and inadequate; especially if we allow ourselves to fall into the sinful pit of comparison and competition.

Making the Wrong Comparison

What if you live next door to a "Martha Stewart"—a woman who is the personification of grace in decorating and entertainment? How about when you sit next to the woman in a Bible study group who knows the Bible better than Ruth Graham?

There are many wonderful, positively positive women who inspire and compel us to do better. But when we move beyond "admire" to "compare," then we can run into trouble. Comparing myself negatively to others can turn the weather of my soul gray and drizzly pretty fast. Sure, I wish I were as impeccable as Martha Stewart, as successful as Oprah Winfrey, as saintly as Mother Teresa. These women and many more inspire me. But I've learned that it's important to choose my role models very carefully. If I choose too high an *ideal*, then I'll focus on my inability to measure up.

When it comes to role models, I ask two questions. What does this woman have in common with me? (Can I relate to her on a personal level?) Does she demonstrate godly character— most especially, does she have a servant's heart?

Negative People

Just as positive people can make our lives much fuller, negative people can leave us empty and wanting. Depression is contagious. No, you can't catch it through the water supply, nor is it an airborne pathogen. But, you *can* catch depression through casual contact.

How many times have you been feeling simply fine, only to call a friend to chat for a few minutes and get bombarded with negative vibes? After thirty minutes of your friend's bitter complaints against her insensitive husband, ill-mannered children, and unreasonable co-workers, you find yourself wanting to go into your bedroom, draw the drapes, crawl into bed, and stay there!

Sometimes friends can be a negative drain on our lives unintentionally. When Cynthia was having marital problems, I desperately wanted to be a help to her. She had always been a faithful friend to me, always there when I needed a word of encouragement or a listening ear. Now I felt it was my responsibility to help her. Galatians 6:2 tells us to "bear one another's burdens, and thus fulfill the law of Christ."

Buoyed along with this scriptural mandate, I jumped in with all my heart to help her carry a load much too heavy for her weary shoulders. But somewhere along the way, I crossed the line from being *helpful* to being *enabling*.

Her phone calls became more and more frequent. Many times her calls came while my family was eating dinner, or late at night when I was talking to my husband. My sleep was disturbed as I dreamed about the terrible situation my friend was experiencing. However, I pushed my own needs aside and continued trying to help.

The advice I offered was often disregarded as I listened to the same stories of hurt and betrayal. More and more I found myself entering into my friend's bitterness toward her husband and others who were hurting her.

Steve began to see the unhealthy balance in our relationship. It became more and more apparent that I was becoming a "security blanket" for Cynthia. Our conversations were extremely lengthy, and less and less effective. Finally, I realized that instead of calling on the Lord for her solace, Cynthia was calling on me.

The day Cynthia called to tell me she had bought a new toothbrush was the clincher. At Steve's insistence I told her not to call so often. I felt terrible—like a horrible friend, as though I had betrayed her, as though I had become like others in her life who had hurt her. Yet I had no other choice. I had become a *negative friend* to her because I allowed her—even encouraged her—to depend on me.

Galatians 6:2 does say we should bear one another's burdens, but it doesn't mean we can be "Christ" to that person. We are to sympathize, show mercy and love, not browbeat a fallen friend. But verse five goes on to say, ". . . every man shall bear his own burden" (KJV). If we can help we should, but ultimately the responsibility to carry one's load of problems is left with the individual. The person who is loaded down is to take those problems first—not to a friend, a counselor, or even their pastor—but to the One who can really help, our "Friend who sticks closer than a brother" (Proverbs 18:24, NIV), Christ himself. By allowing my friend to use me as her "savior" I was hurting her rather than helping her. When we try to help to the extent that we take away a person's need for Christ, we are not being a friend—we are being a hindrance.

Positive Words

Words can have a great influence on how we feel. First Thessalonians 4:18 says, "Therefore, encourage each other with these words" (NIV). We can be encouraged ourselves by listening to positive words—for example, the words of a favorite preacher—and we can encourage others by putting a guard over the words we use when we talk about our neighbors. Keep your words free from the negativity of gossip.

Isaiah 61:1–3a says, "The Spirit of the Sovereign Lord is on me, because the LORD has anointed me to *preach* good news to the poor. He has sent me to bind up the brokenhearted, to *proclaim* freedom for the captives and release from darkness for the prisoners, to *proclaim* the year of the LORD's favor and the day of vengeance of our God, to *comfort* all who mourn, and provide for those who grieve in Zion—to bestow on them a crown of beauty instead of ashes, the oil of gladness instead of mourning and a *garment of praise instead of a spirit of despair*" (NIV, emphasis added).

Second Corinthians 10:5 says, "We demolish arguments and every pretension that sets itself up against the knowledge of God, and we take captive every thought to make it obedient to Christ" (NIV).

The battle of the tongue is won not in the mouth, but in the heart.

We do have the ability to encourage or discourage each other with the words we say. In order to maintain a positive mood, our hearts must be in good condition. We exercise our bodies to build strength. We give strength to our souls as we train ourselves to speak words of thankfulness and praise.

Staying Mentally Alert

A friend of mine who has several children told me her husband criticizes her for being late too often. He said, "You need to be more organized. Your problem is you lack organization skills." Her response rang true to me. She said, "In order to be organized, you have to be able to put two thoughts together. With these children, I haven't had a complete thought in over six years. My biggest problem isn't a lack of organization; my biggest problem is that I've forgotten how to think."

When life is absolutely crazy, and so are we, where do we go to find mental alertness? The place to start is in seeing what the Word of God has to say about learning to think the way He wants us to think. The book of James provides some wonderful instruction concerning keeping a good mental balance. In this world where we are bombarded by mental assaults at every turn, we need positive help on how to think and how to make good decisions. "But if any of you lacks wisdom, let him ask of God, who gives to all men generously and without reproach, and it will be given to him" (James 1:5).

When our minds are renewed daily, we then have new and positive things to think on. We don't need to dwell on hurts and burdens from the past. Laying aside those things, both the good and the bad, we press on toward new and greater aspirations. God renews our minds and gives us new and exciting challenges to face.

What is one of the major hindrances to staying mentally alert? *We overload our minds with things to do that may not be what God wants us to do.* Regardless of the season of our lives, the temptation to do too much always looms over us.

Is Overdoing It Undoing You?

My dad always used to say, "You can work a willing horse to death." I've been the willing horse that is just about ready for the old glue factory. As I get older, and hopefully wiser, I have chosen a new lifetime motto: "Just because you can, doesn't mean you should."

Saying no is a risky thing to do. In the music business, if you say no to work opportunities, sooner or later people stop calling. Given this, one is tempted to say yes every time someone calls for a music session, a television appearance, a radio interview, or recording possibility. The same is true for other businesses. You've heard it said, "Opportunity knocks once, so you'd better open the door." In our pressure-cooker society, is it any wonder that we find ourselves "steamed and ready to blow"?

In order to stay mentally alert (more commonly known as mentally sane), we must learn to say *no*. Here are a few ways we can do this:

1. *Say no politely but firmly.* You can say no and still be a nice person. There is no need to hurt anyone's feelings when you say no; however, there is no need to say yes and end up overloaded. Express thanks for being considered capable of the task or the position being offered, and offer a short explanation as to your situation.

2. *Stand your ground with manipulative people.* Be aware that some people are expert manipulators (even, I'm sad to say, some church leaders) and can get you to say yes when you had every intention of saying no. One effective method of manipulation is the "silent treatment." By the time you have countered their silence with all your reasons for not doing what they want, your reasons have begun to sound like excuses and you give in after all. (We Christians don't want to appear as if we're making excuses to avoid doing "the Lord's work.") If you find yourself feeling guilty for saying no, be wary: You may be in the clutches of an expert manipulator! Don't let anyone else "push your buttons" and get you to agree to things you know you haven't got time or energy for.

3. *Say no through your actions.* If your week has gone awry, skip the band booster meeting. You can pick up the minutes from a friend. We don't always have the time and energy to do everything we would like. Remember, *just because you can doesn't always mean you should!*

Don't answer the phone if it's not convenient for you. There's no reason to interrupt your relaxing hot bath by diving for the phone in the next room—leaving a trail of soapy water across your carpet. "But what if it's an emergency?" you say. Never mind. They'll call back. By choosing to answer only when it's convenient, you have taken back some control over your life. Answering machines or voice mail can help keep life from becoming overwhelming. When you don't want to talk on the phone, let your machine say, "No, I can't come to the phone right now." Here's a hint: Let the machine answer when you *are* home. You can screen your calls, picking up and answering when it really is important. Then, when you leave the house, turn the machine off. That way you don't have to return calls when you get home. If someone really wants to get ahold of you, they will call back.

4. *Don't say maybe when you really mean no.* People pleasing is a hazardous job. When we fear the opinions of others, we can sometimes want and need to say no, but find it easier to say maybe. When we do this we mislead the person asking, and we do harm to ourselves. Be honest: Let your yes be yes and your no be no. (See Matthew 5:37.)

In order to stay mentally alert, we must also learn when to say *yes*:

1. *Say yes to help.* Galatians 6:2 says, "Bear one another's burdens, and thus fulfill the law of Christ." Too often we read this verse and look around to see if there is anyone who needs our help. I want to challenge you to read this verse in light of allowing others to help carry *your* burden. Learn to ask for help. Not only will you have more energy for the task you need to do, but perhaps you will be able to help others also.

2. *Say yes to accepting limits.* My friend Janice went to the doctor totally exhausted. Fortunately, her doctor is a Christian who was able to give her wise advice. He told her, "Janice, there is no way you can please everybody, so don't even try. The only Person you have to please is God. After Him, your next obligation is to your husband, and then to yourself. If you try to please everyone, you'll end up in the hospital." Accepting the fact that we are limited women, with limited energy, can be liberating. Doing only what God has called us to do is the place to start in simplifying priorities.

3. *Say yes to personal time with God.* Spending time alone with the Lord is essential to staying mentally alert. Finding this time is very difficult, especially when you have small children. The minute you wake up in the morning, their little radars are activated like heat-sensing missiles. When that happens, don't be discouraged. You may regret that you don't have the quality devotional block of time that perhaps you had established before the children came along. But be assured that God does hear the

cry of a mother's heart as she calls out for help and comfort.

Even those of us with older children can find it difficult to set aside quality devotional time. Perhaps you are a mother who must hold down a full-time job outside the home, or you are involved in volunteer and church activities, or you home-school your children. Whatever your situation, you may be finding it difficult to spend time alone with God. The pressures of our lives pull us in so many directions that it is indeed difficult to get our minds and bodies to settle down and be quiet before the Lord. Ask God for help. He knows your situation and will help. Be thankful for unexpected opportunities to be alone. Use those times to let your mind dwell on God's goodness.

Keeping Energy Levels High

Rest is not an option. For our bodies and minds to function as God intended, we need to allow ourselves time for rest and refreshment. God gave us clear instruction in the Ten Commandments to set aside one day a week for rest: "Thou shalt keep the Sabbath day holy." Yet this seems to be one commandment that in our busy world we find difficult to obey. Why is it when it comes to maintaining a day of rest that we throw even the mere possibility out the window? Somehow, it seems downright un-American to have a day when we are nonproductive. Is Sunday a day of rest for you and your family? Is there *any* day that you consider a day of rest?

My sister-in-law Jeannie Martin, a pastor's wife and mother of three grown children, shared her thoughts on keeping a day of rest:

> Most people would think that Sunday is not a day of rest for the pastor's family, given all the responsibilities required at church. But, looking back, Sunday was our favorite day of the week.
>
> On Sunday morning I'd get up at 6:00 A.M. and put our dinner in the oven. Then when we came home from church, I could have dinner ready in ten or fifteen minutes. We hardly ever went out to eat on Sunday. This was and still is a time for our family to enjoy being together.
>
> We never went to the malls or shopping on Sunday. It's not that I felt it was some terrible sin, and it's not a doctrinal belief of our church, but this is how our family chose to

celebrate the Lord's Day. It was and is important for us to have a day of rest.

My daughter, Tammi, and I would do the dishes. This gave us some time together—time she may have just as soon done without! When the children were small, I'd put them down for a nap. As they got older, they went to their rooms to rest. They were required to do homework *before* Sunday. My husband, Gene, would sleep for half an hour and then go back over to the church office and prepare his heart for the evening service. The quietness of an empty church was restful to him, while I preferred a nice nap.

Not long ago, I asked our children what they remembered about Sundays. My oldest son, now married with two children of his own, said what he remembered was how calm the day seemed. Tammi, who is also married, said she remembered doing dishes, (ha!) but then she said, "Sundays were great! They were so calm. I really felt rested by the end of the day."

Todd, who is still living at home, said, "I love Sunday. I love getting up from the dinner table and having no oxygen to my brain because I eat too much. Everything is real calm."

All three of my children used the word "calm" when referring to Sundays.

We've chosen to avoid bringing home guests from church on Sundays. If an evangelist is preaching at our church, then the church cooks the meal. Of course, there will be times when the routine is interrupted, but I refuse to let the exception become the norm.

Because we put some boundaries around our day of rest and protected it diligently, when our family went back to church on Sunday evenings we were refreshed. The rest of the congregation had been flopping around at the mall all afternoon, but the preacher and his family were ready to worship.

Even though most of the children are gone now, I still love Sundays. Sometimes Gene will say, "Oh, honey, don't cook. We'll go out." And I'll say, "No. When I planned my grocery shopping, I got the dinner for Sunday." I find it more restful to eat at home on Sunday. As a day of rest, it is too important for me to give up. I need it.

I have personally tried making Sunday a day of rest either by eating at home as a family or by eating out. We enjoy both. When the children were small, it made more sense to come home and eat. There was nothing restful in trying to keep children quiet in a room filled with people wanting to relax. A peanut butter sandwich in peace is better than the finest steak when your gut is in a knot.

Whether you go out to eat or stay home, the most important part is to connect with your family while you have a time set aside for rest and refreshing. Keeping a day of rest will refuel your depleted energies and help you cope better with the entire week.

Planning Ahead

Preventing a breakdown makes much more sense than trying to put the broken pieces back together. A very difficult week is something for which to plan ahead. Many times there are warning signs to help prepare for those stressful, difficult times. There are other times, however, when you can be absolutely blindsided, when you are caught totally off guard. When those times pop up, take mental notes, call out to God for help, and strive for survival.

The week I described at the beginning of this chapter was a time I knew I was going to be busy, but I didn't realize I was not physically up for that kind of stress. PMS had reared its ugly head, and so everything else was magnified by my being in a physically weakened state.

If you know a crunch is coming, then prepare for it:

1. *Make sure to get enough sleep.*
2. *Eat sensibly.* Eat a balanced diet so you won't feel so deprived. It's a terrible strain to be both stressed and deprived of basic nourishment.
3. *Reschedule whatever you can.* Make an effort to remove yourself from any added stress. Arrange for your husband and children to take over some of the household duties. If you include your family ahead of time, and they understand the situation, they will soon realize it is in their best interests to help. Around our house the popular saying is, "When Mama ain't happy, ain't nobody happy!"
4. *Ask a friend to help with any errands you can delegate.* Promise to do the same for her when she is in a similar situation.

Just Do It!

In fairness, exercise should be part of keeping our energy levels high, but who has time to exercise? I was watching TV (don't worry, I'm sure I was ironing or folding clothes at the same time) and a movie star was telling how she relieves stress and keeps in shape. "Just work out for three to four hours daily." Yeah, right! I don't have time to go to the bathroom on a regular basis, and I'm supposed to find three to four "extra" hours in my day? My response to her is, "Get real!"

Even if we can't invest that kind of time (or money) to get our bodies fit, the truth is, no matter how much we may resist the idea of exercise and find excuses not to do it, it probably is one of the *best* ways to build our energy levels and help us function more efficiently. God made our bodies for movement, and human beings have succeeded in finding multiple methods of managing life without movement—sitting at computers for hours a day, driving around in cars, letting escalators and elevators do our climbing for us. . . . The net result of all these labor-saving devices, designed to make our lives easier and more productive, seems instead to be making us more stressed out and on the losing side of the great Battle of the Bulge.

The good news is, we don't have to spend great chunks of time each day exercising in order to reap tremendous benefits. Even five minutes a day, working up to fifteen to twenty minutes a day (not three to four hours), can build stamina within two weeks. Nor do we have to invest in expensive exercise equipment or personal trainers. A good pair of walking shoes may be all we need to get started. A brisk daily walk can work wonders for our energy level and mental outlook. Don't you owe it to yourself (and your family) to do at least that much?

If you are one of the millions of Americans who has not yet established a habit of regular exercise—despite all the pleas in recent years of the medical profession and health enthusiasts— then try these suggestions:

1. *Ask your doctor for advice.* An important first step is to get sound medical advice, including an overall physical exam, to find out what kind of exercise is appropriate for your age, weight, and general state of health.

2. *Start slowly and build up very gradually.* Even if you feel you aren't accomplishing very much, your body will begin to re-

spond positively to regular exercise. Be patient and believe that good results will come from your efforts.

3. *Keep your expectations realistic.* A daily walk around the block won't make you lose twenty pounds in a month, but it *will* make you feel better and will start building those atrophied muscles and getting them used to movement. You may even find that getting out for a few minutes each day to enjoy some fresh air, sunshine, and brisk movement becomes so invigorating that you'll want to do more and more!

There are plenty of up-to-date books on the market, too, with the latest research about the benefits of exercise that can help you get started. *Overcoming the Dieting Dilemma* by Neva Coyle, and *The All-New Free to Be Thin* by Neva Coyle and Marie Chapian[1] offer excellent advice on exercise as well as weight management.

Is Exercise Enough?

As helpful as exercise is, it isn't the sole answer to keeping our energy levels high. We need to have a look at some of our other habits that might be causing us unneeded stress and weariness. Examine your own situation and ask yourself what things about your life are depleting your energies. Can you make changes? Write your ideas down. Here are a few suggestions to get you started:

1. *Eat high-energy foods.* Do your best to keep away from high-fat, high-calorie, low-nutrient foods. This in itself can give you a lift. Eating heavy, fat-laden foods can give you the feeling of having just ingested an anvil. That Snickers bar may taste great and satisfy you momentarily, but an apple will provide important nutrients and give you long-lasting energy.

Fats and starchy foods (like pasta salad), unaccompanied by a protein, increase the brain's production of serotonin, a chemical that can make you sleepy. This is great on vacation, but not so helpful when you need to stay alert and active.

2. *Make a to-do list.* My sister Gayle is an extremely busy

---

[1]Neva Coyle, *Overcoming the Dieting Dilemma* (Minneapolis, Minn.: Bethany House Publishers, 1991).
Neva Coyle and Marie Chapian, *The All-New Free to Be Thin* (Minneapolis, Minn.: Bethany House Publishers, 1993).

woman. Juggling all the demands of being a wife, the mother of three school-age children, a preschooler, and an infant, as well as volunteering at the Crisis Pregnancy Center, serving as den-mother for Cub Scouts, and a host of other school and church responsibilities, she has found that making a to-do list is the best way to get her work done. Even when unexpected tasks pop up that demand her immediate attention, she adds them to her list and crosses them off when completed. "At the end of my busy day," she says, "I can see that I have accomplished something, even if it was not on my initial list of things to do."

3. *Take a short nap.* Fifteen to twenty minutes of rest can rejuvenate your mind and body. Longer periods of rest, however, can have the opposite effect, making you feel more tired and groggy.

If you can't nap, then take a few minutes to sit quietly and relax. You'll get more done with the rest of your day if you stop occasionally for a breather.

4. *Change activities.* At times I have so much to do that I panic and use up valuable energy worrying that I'll never get it all done. If part of your pressure-schedule is to call seventy-five band moms and remind them to turn in the money from the magazine sale, then pace yourself. Make ten calls; then get up and answer a letter, have a cup of tea, or do some laundry. Set a timer to remind you to go back to the phone. A change may be all you need to keep the panic button deactivated.

5. *Set aside some "me" time.* Ask your husband to take over with the children's bedtime routine. If you're a single mom (or your husband can't or won't help with this), turn the TV off and start the nighttime process earlier than usual. Putting the children to bed at a leisurely pace can help take the panic out of it. After they're tucked in bed, take a long, hot bath. Light a candle, put on some relaxing music, or play a tape of Scripture readings, and set the mood for a peaceful night's sleep.

6. *Get enough sleep.* Psalm 127:2 says, "It is vain for you to rise up early, to retire late, to eat the bread of painful labors; for He gives to His beloved even in his sleep." If you have times when you miss sleep—because of a sick child, or an interrupted schedule, or jet lag—then return to your regular sleep schedule as soon as you can. Sleep experts say that we can't really "catch up" on missed sleep by sleeping in. But we'll feel rested if most

of the time we stick to regular sleep hours—going to bed and getting up at the same time every day. When that pattern gets interrupted, it's important to get back to it as soon as possible.

If a certain task is keeping you up late, then go to bed and finish the job in the morning rather than miss your regular sleep.

Take an honest look at your sleep patterns. Are they regular, and if not, can you do something about it? If you fail to maintain adequate rest you may get sick, or simply find your ability to cope with everyday life impaired. (That's a polite way of saying that you'll be a real grouch if you don't get enough sleep!)

7. *Concentrate on the situation at hand.* Like a marathon runner, if you are constantly dwelling on the miles yet to run, you will become overwhelmed and lose heart.

If that "inner alarm" is sounding, step back. Look at what you've done, and refuse to think about what's yet to come.

8. *Spend some time alone with the Lord.* Reading His Word, praying . . . unloading our pressures and asking Him to refresh our minds and hearts will also help to keep our energy levels intact.

Matthew 11:28–30 gives us the very best advice to the woman who is overworked and overwhelmed: "Come to Me, all who are weary [who work to exhaustion] and heavy-laden, and I will give you rest. Take My yoke upon you, and learn from Me, for I am gentle and humble in heart; and you shall find rest for your souls. For My yoke is easy and My load is light."

If the load you're carrying is breaking your back (and mind), then ask yourself two questions: First, is this the load the Lord has intended me to carry, or is this something I've taken on myself? And second, am I willing to allow Him to help shoulder the load?

Go ahead and make the trade. His yoke is easy; His load is light. He's big enough for the task.

4

I Know I Love My Family . . . I Just Can't Remember Why

Do you ever find this thought running through your mind? I do! It usually creeps up on me in moments of total chaos when my coping skills are especially weak. And it's in those times that the phrase "thankless job" slips in there, too.

My friend Laura admits she hears the same phrase in her head. Recently, her husband, John, had to leave for a week-long business trip. With four children under five—one of them a two-month-old—and with no outside help, it was going to be very difficult on Laura. She bolstered herself in prayer, kept a cheerful attitude, and posted the number for pizza delivery on the refrigerator. During the five days of testing, she gathered strength from the Lord. Laura had the children in church Sunday morning and evening, and also on Wednesday evening. Somehow she managed to survive the days without resorting to use the television as a babysitter. She kept her home in impressive running order.

As the time approached for John's return from his grueling days of boring meetings—and thrilling ballgames and fine restaurants—Laura anticipated a lovely family reunion. When the day arrived, Laura worked herself to exhaustion to make everything special for their blessed reunion. The house was given an extra "run through" and was in perfect order (well, as perfect as four little children will allow). Dinner was simmering on the stove—a pot roast and veggies (his favorite). The three little girls were all dressed alike with hair ribbons in place, while big brother sat, hair combed and clean-faced, patiently waiting for Daddy to return. In the closet, where no one noticed, were freshly laundered, starched white shirts ready for the next week.

Looking back over the seemingly undoable task, Laura felt pretty good. "I didn't even cry once during the week," she said, "not that I didn't feel like it."

The time arrived, but John didn't. An airplane delay was not factored into Laura's schedule. Even though the children grew restless, somehow Laura was able to hold it together for a few extra hours. One of the little girls fell asleep, but there were still enough hugs waiting for Daddy. As John walked into the house, he went straight to the children to give and receive the longed-for hugs and kisses. He didn't notice the clean house, the children became quickly disheveled, and his comment about dinner had something to do with fat content and that he had decided to start watching his weight. The romantic conversation that evening between Laura and John was along the lines of, "You wouldn't believe what a hard week I've had. I got so sick of sitting in meetings. I was bored out of my mind." The real clincher came when John confessed his deep hurt and disappointment that she and the children had not come to the airport to greet him at the gate. The dinner and the immaculate house were not even mentioned. After all she had done, it seemed she had not done enough.

Let's face it. Sometimes our families drain us dry. Then they want more. At that point, love is a choice. As I talked to Laura the day after the "family reunion" she said, "I have learned that a person cannot depend on someone else's affirmation. I did a good job. I believe I have gained the Lord's approval, and He definitely proved His faithfulness to me. That's the best I can count on." I was very impressed that Laura was able to dismiss her husband's insensitivity and not take it personally. She was quick to acknowledge that he had had a pretty hard week. I, on the other hand, was quick to point out that conducting peace negotiations between the Palestinians and the Jews would be a Sunday school picnic compared to taking care of four preschoolers all week without a husband's love, help, and support. Even with my thoughtless prodding, she would not slip into the pit of self-pity. My admiration for her soared! I was even more impressed with her spiritual strength to look to the only One who could confirm and affirm her work as wife and mother, than with her ability to hold it together all week. Though no one else saw those clean shirts in the closet, the One who ultimately will confer her job evaluation on this earth saw every ironed shirt.

Is there a more thankless job on the face of this earth than being a mother who stays at home with her children? In the last few decades, women who have chosen their home as their career and nurturing their children as their main focus have been publicly maligned and privately shunned. Social gatherings, where a woman's worth is not only evaluated by the size of her waist but also by the depth of her résumé, can make a stay-at-home mom easily feel misjudged and devalued. She doesn't need it reinforced to her that her career offers little in monetary advancement or health benefits, and that little of what she accomplishes is visible at the end of her day. But just like Laura's ironed shirts hidden in the closet, what a mother at home is doing, or is *not* doing, will be revealed in time. A mother's time with her children is not a short-term loan, but a lifetime investment.

A Mother's Calling: Success Is Not Found in Numbers but in Obedience

Philip was in the middle of a great revival. Chapter 8 in the book of Acts tells us that great and miraculous things were taking place under his ministry. No doubt about it—Samaria was the "happening" place to be. Word was getting out that fabulous results were being witnessed: many salvations, the casting out of unclean spirits, and healings of all sorts. The Holy Spirit had fallen on Samaria. I'm sure Philip felt extremely fulfilled and excited to be an intricate part of this historical event in the life of the Church.

But right in the middle of all this wonderful ministry, something strange happened. The Lord sent an angel and told Philip, "Arise and go south to the road that descends from Jerusalem to Gaza." Verse 26 continues to say in parentheses, "This is a desert road." I wonder if this sounded strange to Philip. In the midst of a great revival, the chief preacher and revivalist is sent to a desert road. There is no indication that Philip argued with the Lord. It simply says in verse 27, "And he arose and went."

If you are familiar with the Scripture to which I am referring, you know there was an Ethiopian eunuch, a court official of Candace, Queen of the Ethiopians, on the desert road. He was the trusted servant who was in charge of the queen's treasure, and had come to Jerusalem to worship. As the eunuch was sitting reading from the prophet Isaiah, the Spirit of the Lord said to Philip, "Go up and join this chariot."

Philip ran up to the man and asked him a simple question: "Do you understand what you are reading?" The man indicated that he would welcome some instruction. Gloriously, the Ethiopian gave his heart and life to Christ and was baptized there on the spot. As the man came up out of the water, Philip was supernaturally snatched away.

With the advantage of history on our side, we know that the Ethiopian eunuch went back to Ethiopia and started the Christian church there, which remained strong through the centuries, even to this day. Philip was unaware of the enormous impact his obedience had on Christendom. But we know his obedience to leave a place of importance, forfeit the affirming accolades of the masses, and go to the desert—where he ministered to one man—had far-reaching effects for generations to follow.

Moms who choose to stay at home and invest their time, energy, and resources in their children and homes need support and honor. Just as Philip chose obedience over applause, a woman who embraces the sometimes thankless job of mothering will positively influence not only her own children, but also the generations to come. I've heard it said we can't do anything about our ancestors, but we *can* do something about our descendants. Even though so much of the work of a mother is unseen (and quickly undone), the long-range effect of a faithful, devoted mother cannot be adequately evaluated.

A six-year-old came home from school one day with a note from his teacher in which it was suggested that he be taken out of school because he was "too stupid to learn." His name was Thomas Alva Edison. In Hebrews 13:2 we are instructed, "Do not neglect to show hospitality to strangers, for by this some have entertained angels without knowing it." This same warning can be applied to mothers: "Beware! That little 'angel' you're caring for may be a part of a bigger plan." This thought is echoed through a song written by Steve:

The Highchair[1]

Who is that little fellow
With ketchup on his nose
Spaghetti in his hair
And a Kodak pose?

Who's sitting in that highchair
Keeping rhythm with a spoon?
Who's got your full attention
And you're crazy as a loon?

Well, he might be the doctor
Who finally finds the cure;
Or the one who leads schools back into prayer;
Or the one who'll be your friend
When you're old and all alone;
You don't know who's sitting in that highchair.

Who is that little lady,
Charming as a lamb,
Painting like an artist
With that pudding in her hands?

Who's sitting in that highchair
With her supper on the floor?
Who's got you saying things
Like "I can't take it anymore"?

She might be the first lady
To fly beyond the moon;
Or the one who changes history with her prayers;
Or she might be there with you
When you're old and all alone;
You don't know who's sitting in that highchair.

Step back, take a look;
Take a picture of this moment in your mind;
That dirty face, in heaven's book
Is where the future treasures always seem to hide.

---

[1]Words and music by Steve Chapman, as recorded on *A Mother's Touch* CD (Times and Seasons Music, Inc., BMI, 1994). Used by permission.

He might be the doctor, who finally finds the cure;
Or she might change history with her prayers;
Or they may be there with you
When you're old and alone;
You don't know who's sitting in that highchair.

A Mother's Choice: Who Will Raise Our Children?

Bob and Sue had a very effective ministry with the youth of the church. Everyone loved them and admired their dedication to the work of the Lord. With both of them working hard they were able to buy a nice house and get on their feet financially before they started a family. Everything was going on schedule.

Eventually God blessed them with a precious baby girl. A few weeks after the birth I inquired of Sue how everything was going. "Oh, everything's fine," she said with a bit of a sigh. "We're really enjoying our daughter. . . . I just wish I had more time to spend with her. She's been in a day-care center since she was six weeks old. By the time I get home from working at the church, there's just enough time for dinner, laundry, and putting her down for the night."

I felt my blood pressure rising as I contemplated how to respond. I wanted to scream, "This isn't right!" Why did this young mother feel that "God's work" at the church was more important than staying home to mother her newborn infant? The tone of her voice betrayed her true feelings—she would have much preferred being with her daughter. Who gave her those feelings but God himself? Isn't staying home to bring up our children in a quiet and godly atmosphere also doing God's work?

Unfortunately, I missed the opportunity to encourage this young friend to consider her options. Instead, I muttered a weak response and went on.

This is clearly a complicated issue in today's world. With corporate downsizing and many being laid off these days, mothers must sometimes go to work to support their families—at least for a time. I understand these realities, but, nonetheless, I want to urge mothers to consider carefully their reasons for placing their young children in day-care centers rather than enjoying the blessings of staying home for a few years and providing their children the benefits of a mother's nurture and care. If there is any way possible to manage financially, I can't emphasize enough how much blessing I believe God can bring out of such a decision!

Please understand that I'm not talking here to women who are abusive or have problems with addictive behaviors. In such cases, their children may well be better off in the care of trained professionals. But I'm speaking to Christian women who love the Lord and want to honor Him: *Who do you want raising your children?* If not you, why not? And how, then, are you going to decide who will be given that important task? God allows for many creative choices in our lives, but we must make sure we aren't getting our values mixed up with the world's values in this extremely important decision.

Bob and Sue are not bad people. On the contrary, I'm sure they would lay down their lives for their little girl. But like many young couples they may sincerely believe that leaving their child in a day-care center, instead of staying at home with her, will do no harm. In this couple's situation, the nobleness of the work being done for the church added a dimension of acceptability. What could possibly be more important than the work of God? Of course, the work of the Lord is vitally important, but so is the responsibility of nurturing the child the Lord gives to a family. Along with the importance of the work, Bob and Sue may be succumbing to additional outside pressures.

Little by little, one by one, decisions are made. There's the purchase of a house just a little beyond reach. One too many times the old "debt card" (deceptively referred to as a "credit card") is used instead of cash. Before long, "lifestyles of the deeply indebted" (with no way out) are established.

With a backbreaking load of debt and possessions, decisions tend to be made on the basis of the standard of living a couple wishes to maintain, rather than on priority or importance. When the children come along, they are born into a system in which the parents have chosen the pursuit of status and material possessions over the priority of a strong family. Once a standard is established, it's very difficult (and often embarrassing) to go backward.

There are churches that preach that material wealth is an indication of God's blessing on the life of the Christian. Such is the case with Bob and Sue; it would not only be a blow to their economic standing, but also a hit spiritually for Sue to quit her job, sell the house, and buy a smaller one. When we mistakenly equate financial gain with God's blessing in our lives, then the materialistic treadmill rolls on and on. And who are the losers in all of this? We all are! The parents, the children, the Church, and all of society will suffer when children are raised knowing their concerns are somewhere behind country, church, and status.

Laying Down Our Lives

Years ago, a young mother was making her way across the hills of South Wales, carrying her little baby in her arms. Unexpectedly, she found herself in a blinding blizzard. Try as she did, she never made it to her destination alive. When the blizzard had subsided, a rescue team was sent to look for the young mother and her baby. The searchers discovered her body beneath the snow, and to their amazement, they found the child alive.

This mother had taken off all her outer clothing and wrapped it around her baby. She had saved her son's life by an act of unselfish sacrifice. Many years later, that child, David Lloyd George, became the Prime Minister of Great Britain. He was, without question, one of England's greatest statesmen.

Not every mother is called upon to literally lay down her life for her child; however, most of us, if called upon, would do just that. The love between a parent and child is a tremendous force. But love isn't always demonstrated in such dramatic acts of courage and affection. Love must also be worked out on an everyday, consistent basis. When that little baby cries in the middle of the night, a mother does not ask herself if she's tired, or whether she *wants* to get up and change and feed the baby. Her feet hit the floor before her eyes are open. She sacrifices her sleep so that her child can sleep.

No Mom Is Perfect!

If you doubt the truth of this statement, just ask my children. On occasion Heidi threatens to write her own book. A possible title that's been kicked around is *Mommy Dearest II*! The idea that parents are imperfect may be the greatest understatement of history. Even though we know there really are no perfect parents (look at Adam and Eve—and they couldn't even blame their failures on a defective mother!), somehow we all would love to be the exception to the rule. There's no doubt in my mind that if it were possible for me to do all things correctly and to always use my sweet "Caroline Ingalls" tone of voice, I would do so.

No parent who is mentally stable would deliberately leave their child emotionally, spiritually, or physically deficient. But "even if we could do everything perfectly," says Dr. Ray Guarendi, author of *Back to the Family*, ". . . there simply are no guarantees in parenting. What kids become depends a lot on us, but also on the world they experience outside our homes, and on their own personality."[2]

When we get to heaven, not one of us will hear, "Best done, thou good and perfect parent." Our very finest efforts will receive a "well done." Only One did it best—our Heavenly Father—and, as you recall, His children rebelled.

Mistakes Are As Much a Part of Mothering As a Glass of Spilled Milk

Errors in judgment, overreactions, and spiritual lapses are an unfortunate yet realistic part of mothering. Why? Is it because we don't love our children and want to hurt them? Of course not. But we are human, and humans are fallible. However, asking God to bring good from our imperfect human nature can work to the benefit of our children.

Admitting our failures and modeling the "humility of confession" will help them learn the truth of 1 John 1:9: "If we confess our sins, He is faithful and righteous to forgive us our sins and to cleanse us from all unrighteousness."

Humility is an attitude modeled by Christ and espoused as a prerequisite for admittance into the Kingdom of Heaven. Matthew 18:3–4 says, "Truly, I say to you, unless you are converted and become as little children, you shall not enter the kingdom of heaven. Whoever then humbles himself as this child, he is the greatest in the kingdom of heaven."

"Humility" in the Greek denotes *adaptability, moldability, flex-*

---

[2]Dr. Ray Guarendi, "Five Parenting Facts of Life," *McCalls* (April 1991), p. 92.

ibility, and *receptivity.* Setting aside any pretense of knowing it all and doing it perfectly is an essential component of godly parenting. As our children observe an attitude and spirit of humility in us, our example will pave the way for them when they must admit to their heavenly Father their own desperate need for guidance and forgiveness.

Not Then, Not When, But Now!

Dr. Guarendi also states, "Raising kids is a moment-to-moment affair. Each day demands on-the-spot decisions and judgments without the full benefit of all the facts. Keeping up with the 'right now' is work enough for most of us. That is why happy parents say: Parent in the present. Don't look back, except to learn. Don't look ahead, except to plan."[3]

Looking back is a tremendous temptation, especially when our children make decisions or take a path in life that is contrary to everything we've taught them. Engaging in the fruitlessly torturous exercise of "if only" or "I wish I hadn't" can only serve to rob us of the energy to concentrate on the task at hand. We must refuse the temptation to go on another "guilt trip," which will only keep us mired in regret and derail our course of action.

We can do our very best at mothering, but ultimately, the choices our offspring make are their responsibility. When Steve walked away from the Lord and the teachings of the Church, it broke his mother's heart. I'm sure there were those moments when she and Steve's father questioned their parenting skills. However, the problem was not Steve's parents; the problem was Steve's choices. Ultimately, we are all left to answer for our own actions. What was the correct response to Steve's rebellion? His parents, especially his mother, diligently prayed for Steve. Instead of wallowing in the past, they brought the Lord into the present. Many years later Steve wrote these words:

Reachable[4]

There's a boy in his mother's prayers
'Cause lately she's been aware
That he's been drifting too far from the shore.

---

[3]Ibid.
[4]Words and music by Steve Chapman, as recorded on *Reachable* CD (Times and Seasons Music, Inc., BMI, 1992). Used by permission.

And she's beginning to believe
The boy is getting out of reach;
Weary mother, don't you worry anymore

'Cause the boy is reachable;
I know he's reachable,
And to God he's visible,
And all things are possible

'Cause if the Lord can reach His hand of love through time
And touch a cold sinner's heart like mine
The boy is reachable, yes, he's reachable.

Did Steve's parents do everything correctly? They would be quick to tell us they did not. Did they do the best they could at the time? I'm confident they did. Have Steve and I done everything right with our children? Sorry to say, Nathan and Heidi, we haven't. Did we mess up on purpose? No. A thousand times, NO! That's not to say, if I could do some things over, I wouldn't do them differently. I would love to go back and redo the times when I made a big deal out of childish pranks, or let out a bloodcurdling scream when they ran over my heel with the shopping cart, or got angry with Nathan when he brought home a bad grade from school. (A lot of good it did to yell at him after the fact.) I regret letting my own fatigue (or PMS) make me a grouch to my children. But, the truth is, I can't change a thing. Learning from these experiences instead of reliving them is the best way to handle our less-than-perfect parenting.

Looking ahead can be just as big a distraction from mothering as looking back. I have dreaded the teen years since my children were infants. I'll never forget holding Nathan on my lap as a sleepy little toddler and saying, "Will you love Mommy when you're sixteen?" For some reason age sixteen always seemed rather ominous to me.

His little-boy reply still rings in my ears: "Oh yes, Mommy, I'll always love you." I only wish I had captured that confession on tape.

Those little-boy years have come and gone. Nathan is now six foot two: two hundred pounds of "godly young man." The teenage years I feared have come and are nearly gone. I wonder how much time and energy I wasted with useless worrying.

Regardless of the issue at hand, mothering is a job for the *present*. We must refuse to borrow sorrow from tomorrow. Matthew 6:34 says, "Therefore do not be anxious for tomorrow; for tomorrow will care for itself. Each day has enough trouble of its own."

Bathe each day in prayer! Trying to carry the weight of tomorrow with today's grace will clip your wings and keep you from soaring. Getting on top and staying on top of this challenging job of mothering can help us love our children on the days when it's easy to love them, and also on the days when it seems impossible. Either way, God's grace is there for us, and it is always sufficient.

Loving Till It Hurts

In the popular *Good Housekeeping* column "Here's Erma," Erma Bombeck shares some of her feelings about being a mother. Her comments reinforce my own belief that motherhood is not for the faint of heart.

Erma says that if she had remained childless her life would have continued, but she would have missed so much. She says, ". . . every Mother's Day I reflect on what I might have been had I not had children. I might have had a waist. But then, it's not all that big a deal to have an indentation to hang a belt on.

"I would probably be more independent than I am. Thanks to my children, I have never gone to the bathroom by myself, driven in a car alone, had my teeth cleaned without an audience, or had a private phone conversation.

"There is no doubt that I would have been more popular. I cannot imagine a childless life earning me as many *I hate you's* and *Why can't you be like everyone else's mother!*"[5]

Yes, to be a mother, it helps to have skin as thick as a groundhog. If we take every careless comment or roll of the eyes personally, we will be on an emotional roller coaster ride to the grave.

Another element of a mother's love is the willingness to discipline her children. Proverbs 20:11 states, "Even a child makes himself known by his acts, whether what he does is pure and right"(RSV). Also, Proverbs 22:15: "Folly is bound up in the heart of a child, but the rod of discipline drives it far from him" (RSV).

---

[5]Erma Bombeck, "Here's Erma," *Good Housekeeping* (May 1993).

A touching story is told of a mother during World War I. Having lost both her husband and son in the fields of Flanders, this woman was overcome with bitterness and grief. Each day she watched as her neighbor enjoyed her large family, for her five sons had been spared while this widowed mother was left all alone.

One night she had a dream. In the dream an angel appeared to her and said that she could have her son back for ten minutes. At what period of his life she wished him to return was strictly up to the mother. The angel asked if she wanted her son back as a tiny babe in her arms nursing at her breast. Or did she want him as a chubby-cheeked toddler playing at her feet? Or as a young boy starting school, as a youth finishing his courses in school, or as a young soldier in his brave new uniform? The choice was hers.

The mother thought for a while and then replied, "I want him back, but in none of these occasions. I think I would like best his return when once I denied his request and remained firm in spite of his insistence. He, in a fit of anger, cried out, 'I hate you—don't like you anymore, and I won't stay with you!' Then he rushed away into the garden. When his anger had abated, he came back to me, his grimy, wistful face stained with tears, and he held out his little arms and with quivering lips said, 'Muvver, I'm so sorry I was naughty boy. I won't be bad anymore ever. I love you and want you to hug me again.' Give him back to me and let me feel him clinging close to me while he sobs his little heart out in sorrow and love. That's when I loved him best."

Being willing to be "hated" because we love our children is as much a part of showing love to them as are all the kisses and hugs we give them for proper emotional development. I stumbled onto a poem (thanks to my sister Alice) that should be words of comfort to mothers everywhere. It helps to know that we are not alone.

I Loved You Enough

Someday when my children are old enough to understand the logic that motivates a mother, I will tell them:

I loved you enough to be silent and let you discover that your handpicked friend was a creep.

I loved you enough to make you return a Milky Way (with a bite out of it) to a drugstore and confess, "I stole this."

I loved you enough to stand over you for two hours while you cleaned your room—a job that would have taken me fifteen minutes.

I loved you enough to let you see anger, disappointment, disgust, and tears in my eyes.

I loved you enough to let you stumble, fall, and hurt.

I loved you enough to say I was sorry and ask for your forgiveness.

I loved you enough to let you assume the responsibilities for your actions at six, ten, and sixteen.

But most of all I loved you enough to say "No!" when you hated me for it. That was the hardest part of all.

This unnamed author had to be a mother who understood the hazards of mothering. She was also a mother who had experienced those scathing words "I hate you!" and loved her child enough to know that sometimes love really does hurt and that parenting isn't a popularity contest.

Teaching our children proper behavior is essential in fulfilling our scriptural responsibility toward our children. If we fail to teach them to obey, then what may seem like love is actually one of the worst things we can do to our children.

In the book *Mothers and Sons* by Jean Lush (Fleming H. Revell, 1994), the author relates a story every mother should hear. She tells of a town surrounded by forests, which were inhabited by dangerous dragons. One day a villager found a baby dragon in the woods. The creature seemed so cute and helpless that the man took him back home. No one thought this little dragon would grow up to be mean and dangerous.

As the dragon grew, so did his appetite. Every day he demanded more and more food. Before long the dragon was breathing fire and the villagers were afraid to refuse his demands.

Eventually the dragon destroyed everything and everyone in the village. And then he destroyed himself.[6]

As mothers, we look down at our tiny bundle of sweet joy and softness. We sigh. Here is undoubtedly the most precious of all creation. True enough, all babies are beautifully marvelous.

---

[6]Original author unknown.

However, it is a wise mother who will love that child enough to recognize that this same little cherub, if left without structure, limits, and control, will turn out to be a "dangerous monster." Giving a child everything he wants is not showing love; it's grooming trouble. Proverbs 23:13 clearly warns overly permissive parents: "Do not hold back discipline from the child, although you beat him with the rod, he will not die. You shall beat him with the rod, and deliver his soul from Sheol." Verses 15 and 16 go on to say, "My son, if *your* heart is wise, *my* own heart also will be glad; and *my* inmost being will rejoice, when *your* lips speak what is right" (emphasis added).

When the Lord gave us our children, it seemed we would always have babies. It has not turned out that way at all. Now we have big adultlike people walking around the house . . . EATING!! Just about the time I think I've got this "mothering" thing figured out, the kids change. It is essential that we keep alert and change with them.

A Mother's Ministry: For Here and Eternity

It was once said that when Robert Moffat, the well-known missionary, was added to the Kingdom of God, a whole continent was added with him. And a mother's kiss did it. When Mr. Moffat left home, his mother walked part of the way with him. After a while, it was time for him to walk on alone. His mother asked him for a promise. After protesting that he could not promise something unless he knew what he was promising, his mother assured him that fulfilling this promise was something he could easily do. At that point Robert Moffat promised his mother that he would start each day with God, and close each day with God. The mother then kissed her son and sent him on his way. Mr. Moffat said that his promise to his mother, sealed with her kiss, made him a missionary.

Not only is it important for a mother to nurture and care for her children's physical and emotional needs, it is equally important for a mother to embrace the ultimate purpose and ministry conferred on her the day she gave birth. Leading our children to Christ at an early age is the most loving act we can ever extend to our children.

When Nathan was five years old, we were traveling through Texas on a singing tour. We stopped at a roadside fruit stand to buy something to eat. While there, Nathan reached up to a table and took a sample of orange. As we were traveling on down the road toward our destination, Nathan began to cry. He then confessed that he had "stolen" the orange slice. Both Steve and I knew that the samples of orange were there for the taking. But in Nathan's heart he hadn't taken the orange; he had stolen it. We turned around, drove forty-five miles back to the fruit stand, and stood with Nathan as he confessed his act of thievery. The woman acted a bit confused but graciously told Nathan that she forgave him. As we began our journey back down the road I shared with Nathan once again how Jesus had provided the payment for his sin. He then prayed and asked Jesus to forgive him and to come into his heart.

Heidi became a Christian on an evening when we were just reading the Bible and explaining the plan of salvation as God's love gift to her. She prayed and asked Jesus into her little three-year-old heart. A year later we were talking about Jesus and how He wants to live in our hearts and be the boss of our lives. I asked Heidi if she had ever invited Jesus to come into her heart and be the boss of her life. She looked at me incredulously and said, "Don't you remember? I asked Jesus in my heart in my room when we were reading the Bible." She knew the time and place; that was good enough for me.

Now that the children are older, they have renewed their commitment to Christ at youth camps and revivals. We all need a refreshing and recommitment from time to time, but their initial relationship was established when they were very young.

Many of our great church leaders were led to Christ at the knee of a loving Christian mother. Polycarp, the courageous early church martyr, was converted at nine years of age. Jonathan Edwards, perhaps the mightiest intellect of the American pulpit, was saved at seven. Count von Zinzendorf, the leader of the Moravians, signed his name to this covenant, "Dear Savior, do Thou be mine and I will be Thine!" at four years of age.

Charles Spurgeon, who was converted at age twelve, said, "A child of five, if properly instructed, can as truly believe and be regenerated as an adult." Griffith John, an effective missionary to China who came to know Christ at age eight, said, "Had I not taken that step then, I doubt whether I should ever have been a missionary, if a member of a Christian church at all." And R.A. Torrey said, "It is almost the easiest thing in the world to lead a child from five to ten years of age to a definite acceptance in Christ."

Mothers, we have the greatest opportunity at hand. Leading our children to Christ should be at the top of our mission and prayer list.

I'm Not Too Young[7]

I'm not too young to sin;
I'm not too young to die;
I'm not too young to begin
A life of faith and joy.

I'm not too young to know
The Savior's love for me
In coming down to earth below
To die upon the tree.

I'm not too young to love;
I'm not too young to pray,
To look to Jesus up above
And all His Word obey.

Jesus, I love Thy name;
From evil set me free,
And ever keep Thy little lamb
Who puts his trust in Thee.

Bob Pittman, a creator and former chairman of MTV, has long understood the power of television and its ability to influence the lives of our children. "The strongest appeal you can make . . . is emotionally. If you can get their emotions going, [make them] forget their logic, you've got 'em. At MTV, we don't shoot for the fourteen-year-olds; we own them."[8]

Not only are our teenagers at risk. "Get them while they're young and the younger the better" is the battle cry of the enemy. As your young children sit in front of Saturday morning cartoons and digest a steady diet of occultic characters and practices, don't be deceived. The crafty Evil One knows what he's doing. As your children ingest a mindful of magic and witches in the very videos Grandma and Grandpa give as Christmas and birth-

---

[7]Paul Lee Tan, *Encyclopedia of 7700 Illustrations* (Rockville, Md.: Assurance Publishers, 1979), p. 234.
[8]As quoted by Bob DeMoss, *Focus on the Family* (August 1994).

day gifts, erroneously assuming that anything with the name Walt Disney on it is wholesome and lovely, open your eyes, Mom. They are not too young to be devoured. They also are not too young to be rescued.

Dr. M.R. deHaan, the well-known Bible teacher, once quoted these startling figures: "After the age of 35 only one person in 50,000 receives Christ; after 45 only one in 300,000; and after 75 only one in 700,000 is converted." Embrace the role of evangelist when it comes to your children.

Deuteronomy 6:4–8 was written to the ancient Hebrews, but the message is just as relevant for us modern-day mothers and fathers: "Hear, O Israel! The LORD is our God, the LORD is one! And you shall love the LORD your God with all your heart and with all your soul and with all your might. And these words, which I am commanding you today, shall be on your heart; and you shall teach them diligently to your sons and shall talk of them when you sit in your house and when you walk by the way and when you lie down and when you rise up. And you shall bind them as a sign on your hand and they shall be as frontals on your forehead. And you shall write them on the doorposts of your house and on your gates."

As you read these verses, think about how your life and home should be reflecting the teachings of the Lord. We are instructed to talk about the things of the Lord when we are at home. At the dinner table, as we watch the evening news, or when a conflict arises, we should be bringing the principles of the Lord into our conversations. When we are making a decision whether or not to buy a car, our children should be a part of the prayer asking God to guide our purchases.

Our daily time with God needs to include more than reading the Bible for five minutes, saying grace at the dinner table, and a few thank-you's at bedtime. Although these prayers are right and good, our devotion to Christ should be reflected in every area of our lives. When you are struggling with a difficult decision, let the children hear you asking for help and guidance. Let your children *see* God opening up opportunities for you and the family. When we seek to make Christ a part of our everyday life, He will then be a familiar friend to our children when we seek to share salvation with them.

We are to wear the symbols of God. Positive T-shirts, plaques, and Scriptures hanging in our home are a constant witness to our children. Words of commitment on our front door saying, "As for me and my house, we will serve the Lord" seem to be in keeping with the spirit of this Scripture. Whatever it takes for our children to know God on an intimate, everyday basis will help in introducing Christ to them as Savior.

However, no amount of "wearing the gospel" will replace the ultimate necessity of "living the gospel" before our children. How we live speaks volumes above anything we could ever say.

No Greater Joy, No Greater Sacrifice

There are mothers today who are choosing the hard road. They are refusing to turn their backs on their children and allow the enemy to devour them body and soul. There's the mom in the inner city that fights the drug pushers. And the mom who sacrifices personal time to be present in the public school classroom, where too often the promoters of "political correctness" have drawn attention away from teaching our children to read and write. Or the mom who chooses to teach her children at home to protect them from the increasing violence, confusion, and godlessness in our schools. These mothers are standing guard to keep wickedness from picking their children's minds clean of godly values and traditions.

The task is never going to be an easy one. We are in a spiritual battle for the lives of our children, and the forces of evil are not going to give up without a fight. The next time you're feeling exhausted, having survived yet another hard day on the home front, perhaps you might be ready to read this poem by J. Mar.

Promise for a Housewife

So you're just a housewife, what a shame,
What fulfillment does that allow you;
For without a business suit, we're told
You're not of any value,
For all you do throughout the day
Is help to shape a life,
And stand in the gap to pray for your home,
And be a godly wife.
You teach your children about the Lord
And His Word as meditation;
So a heritage will follow their lives

From generation to generation.
And when on that final judgment day
The saints gather around His throne;
I wonder how many shall surely say,
"I'm here 'cause Mom stayed home."

Battle on, mothers! The task at hand is worthy of the sacrifice.

5

What Price Success?

All women work. Just ask my friend Molly, who home-schools four of her children and takes care of a toddler and an infant. "There are days," she says, "when going to a job and leaving my children in the care of others would feel like a paid vacation."

There are times when many stay-at-home moms would gladly trade places with their husbands who "get" to go off to their child-free offices five days a week. But "the-grass-is-always-greener" trap is one that's easy to fall into and hard to climb out of once we've made a habit of such wishful thinking. There simply are no easy solutions in this life when it comes to providing our families with their material needs, as well as giving them our undivided attention.

Sometimes we're called upon to make sacrifices we never expected to have to make, and that could include going back to work when we'd really prefer to stay home with our children. A decision for Mom to help provide the family income needs to be made together before God—*and every member of the family must recognize that such a change will require added responsibilities for each of them.* Working mothers simply cannot keep doing all the things they used to do when they were at home all day. Such unrealistic expectations will cause unneeded heartache and pressure for the family—and will undoubtedly lead to exhaustion for Mom.

As mothers, we need to weigh the burdens an outside job may place on our family—and also weigh the possible *benefits* that may accrue as our children (and husbands!) learn to take on more responsibility for the care of the household. Be willing to count the cost and decide if the additional income is truly a "need" or simply a "want" for a higher standard of living. (See *Smart Women Keep It Simple*, "Eliminating Competition," the chapter in which I discuss some of the benefits and drawbacks of working outside the home.)

My friend Adrian reluctantly found herself back in the work force as her youngest child entered school. She wasn't fully prepared for the changes this would bring to her family as she experienced firsthand the exhausting job of trying to keep work and home in balance. With much emotion and many tears she shared her story:

> I have three terrific kids and have stayed home with them until the last couple of years. Since I went back to work (which was not my desire), I have been pushed over my limits in every area of my life. I feel so guilty sometimes because I see all of these mothers that work, and they seem to have it all together. Of course, I know they don't, since I have their children all day in school. I see what these children are missing, and I don't want that for mine.
>
> I feel deeply that I should be at home and available for my children. However, God is using this difficult situation in the life of our family. Because of my going back to work, my husband and I are in marriage counseling after twenty-five years of marriage. Until I went to work I was able to take everything on myself. I felt because I was at home, I could do it all; I could hold it together. My husband never had to deal with his problems, because I was there to buffer any uncomfortable situations. But now with the stress of my working and trying to do things the way I've always done it, I am on the verge of a collapse. I can't be everything to my family, and we're not coping well.
>
> I don't know how well the counseling is going, but at least it's a start. I have come to the conclusion that we have to do something. I have decided to resign this coming year. I'm willing to do whatever it takes. I'm willing to sell the

house and live in a two-room hut. . . . I just want my family back.

Those of us who work both inside and outside of the home understand Adrian's plight all too well—that panicky feeling of running on empty with no exit in sight. That feeling should indeed be a warning signal for us to stop and examine our options. Are we really going about things the way God wants us to? Or have we taken on more responsibility than is reasonable, or is even *possible* for us to cope with? Is God trying to get our attention? The complicated situations that we as working women face may be the very thing God uses to alert us to a problem. Consider this anecdote:

A farmer was having a problem with his mule. The mule had decided to stubbornly plant himself in the middle of the road and refused to budge. A city slicker came by and saw the farmer's dilemma.

"Look," the city slicker chided, "you're doing it all wrong. You must talk to the mule. Reason with him. Use psychology. The problem is not the mule; it's your inept approach to the mule that's the problem."

The farmer, fully aware of the basic stubborn nature of the mule, told the city slicker, "If you know so much, then *you* get the mule out of the road."

The city slicker eagerly took the challenge. As he walked over to the mule, he picked up a two-by-four lying by the side of the road. He went over and cracked that old mule between the eyes.

The farmer protested. "You said you were going to talk to the mule, to reason with him."

The city slicker answered, "I am, but first I needed to get his attention."

Sometimes I feel like that old mule. I'm stuck in the middle of life's highway, about to be run over by my own stubbornness. Sometimes, it is as though God picks up a two-by-four and cracks me between the eyes—just to get my attention.

No time is getting our attention more necessary than in the area of working out the delicate balancing act between being a wage earner and shouldering life's many other responsibilities.

God's "two-by-fours" may vary in their severity and their purpose. It may be anything from a dull headache to a total breakdown, but there are times when getting our attention is where He must start in order to get us out of the middle of the road and on our way toward the prize of the high calling in Christ Jesus. (See Philippians 3:14.) Why is it we have to be "hit" with problems at home—a physical illness, a floundering marriage, or a rebellious child—before we see that we are stuck in the middle of life, paralyzed by problems beyond our control, and even more painful, of our own making?

Life at the Top

At first Alice thought her dream had come true! She had gone as far with the company as possible. After starting at the bottom and working very hard, she had finally arrived in the executive suite. Feeling rather good about her accomplishment, she set out to do the best job possible. It was this attitude that had carried her to the top, and as far as she was concerned, nothing had changed.

Having arrived at the top, however, there was no place else for Alice to go. The challenge was met and the goals were reached. Before she could unpack her pencils and pens, jealousy reared its ugly head. Before the promotion, she had enjoyed an amicable relationship with her fellow workers. Now it was difficult to adjust to their suddenly unfriendly attitudes, and her own feelings of loneliness and rejection became unbearable.

The late hours, the constant office politics, the work she had to take home (or do during her lunch hour), were "unperks" she had not anticipated. Tired feet, hurt feelings, falling asleep during dinner, conflicts at home. . . . Was this the payoff for all the years of struggle? With all the stress of success, Alice realized she was paying a much higher price than the slight raise and private office was worth. She decided to step down—preferring a more manageable life than her new title permitted.

Fortunately for Alice, she was able to return to her old position and let those who jealously clawed and fought for her new job have it. Sometimes the price of success is simply too high.

No Price Too High

Renee had made the decision early in her pregnancy to return to work as soon as the baby was six weeks old. It seemed the logical thing to do, since her mother lived close by and had offered to care for the child while Renee worked. The perfect situation. The baby would remain in its own environment, there would be no break in the schedule, and everyone would be happy.

All Renee's life she had looked forward to teaching elementary school. Everyone told her she was a born teacher and had such a good rapport with children. As the birth of her baby approached, the excitement was overwhelming. Soon the baby arrived, and even sooner it was time to return to her beloved first graders.

Renee was not prepared for the flood of feelings she experienced that first day of teaching. She just couldn't "get back into the swing of things." All she could do was think about her baby. The grief over leaving her child, even in the capable hands of her own mother, was more than she could bear. Twice that first day she called home, crying both times. What was she going to do?

"Give it some time" was the advice everyone seemed to offer. Renee's husband had just started his own business, and her paycheck, the health insurance, and financial cushion was thought to be desperately needed at this time in her family's life.

Since Renee had been raised in a two-paycheck home, she had grown accustomed to the best of everything. Her family was unsure that she would be able to adjust to having so little expendable income if she were to quit her teaching job and come home to be a full-time mom.

Finally, Renee and her husband, Stan, made a decision based not on finances alone but on their priorities as parents. She would come home in order to be a more vital part of her son's first year. Thankfully, her teacher's contract provided for "infant bonding," and she could leave for the year without giving up her teaching position entirely. Maybe in another year Renee will be ready to return to the classroom, but for now she has decided to delay that decision.

The feelings of guilt and grief experienced by women who are torn between the need to earn a wage and the need to be at home with their families can be terribly traumatic. Except for a small number of extreme feminists, women are aware that the most important job they can do is nurture and care for their families. In fact, the modern trend baffling the experts is that, after decades of fighting for entry into the workplace, many women are coming home. Just like Adrian, Alice, Renee, and countless others, women feel a need to work; yet their hearts are divided.

There are three explanations given for this movement back home. First, women are sick and tired of the harried, exhausted, chaotic lifestyle that often characterizes the two-career family. Second, many are realizing that very little money is left over after taxes, child care, and work-related expenses. It is estimated that close to eighty percent of a woman's salary goes for covering these costs. This fact has caused many women to reevaluate whether their salary is worth the price they are paying personally, or is worth the toll it takes on their families. The third reason women are coming home has to do with the present state of the economy. With lower interest rates on mortgages, homes are more affordable, making it more possible for married women to stay at home. The trend toward refinancing homes and the commitment to eliminating unnecessary consumption has also helped make this change possible.[1]

Even with the desire to stay at home, there are lots of women who find it necessary to work outside the home for a variety of reasons.

Making Changes, and Making Sure

Sherry had stayed at home with her children when they were young. She was so happy to be able to give her concentrated effort to providing an atmosphere where her children could always count on her being there for them. Sherry home-schooled, baked her own bread, served in her church, and was extremely involved in every activity of her children. Never did a piano recital, soccer game, or band concert pass by that she was not there on the front seat cheering her children on. Sherry was fulfilling her definition of a "good mom."

It was after her youngest son entered private school that Sherry and her husband, Jason, decided that if they were going to make it financially, Sherry was going to have to go back to work.

Sherry had a master's degree in education but had not taught

[1]*Focus on the Family* newsletter (August 1994).

since before her first son was born. To be certified to teach meant going back to school and renewing her teaching credentials. With Sherry attending college classes, life changed around the house. No longer were there healthy meals waiting for her family as they entered the door from their varied activities. Instead of well-thought-out meals with homebaked whole-wheat bread, they ate leftover spaghetti or Domino's pizza for dinner.

Sherry told me, "I get so depressed. Five years ago, my focus was on my family. I was an absolute health fanatic. I used to eat right and exercise. I was fit and toned in body and mind. Now all that's changed. I get up at 5:00 A.M. Sometimes I don't get home in the evenings until 5:30 or 6:00 P.M. This job of teaching is all-consuming. People don't realize that if you do the job right, it takes all your time. I don't have time for myself or my family.

"I worry about my teenage sons, as well as my youngest. I'm falling apart in every area of my life that I believe in. What am I going to do? I love the Lord, and I love my family; I also feel like the Lord provided this job to help my family. I get really excited about teaching; God has given me a love for it. I keep asking God to help me get control of this job instead of the job controlling me. I don't think I've learned that lesson yet. Is there any hope for me? I feel so stuck. I know I have to keep working; we've all invested far too much in this for me to wimp out now. But I just need to learn how to get my life back into balance and keep it there. I've been at this for five years. I wonder if I'll ever get it right!"

Confessions of Working Women

When we consider the question, "Should women work outside the home?" there is no right or wrong answer. The best we can do is honestly seek God's strength and direction concerning our priorities.

It is normal for working mothers to feel a mix of emotions at times as they juggle so many different responsibilities. Ideally, many mothers would love to be able to stay home and devote all their time and energies to raising their children and being homemakers, but economic realities and other life situations do not always allow for that choice. If you are feeling uncertain about your situation, you are not alone. Listen to what these mothers have to say:

My name is Susan and I have 2.7 children. Yes, I'm pregnant again! Before my first son was born I was determined to work until the day he was born, take my six weeks of maternity leave, place him in day care, and go back to work. I had *something* to prove to *somebody*, but to this day I haven't figured out what or to whom. I wasn't a Christian at the time, and the whole idea of seeking God's will and purpose in my life was pretty foreign. All I knew was I wanted to climb the corporate ladder, make money, and have nice things. But something unexpectedly happened two minutes after Nathan was born. I immediately fell in love with this little wonder. My husband was all for my staying home. He was in favor of my breast-feeding—the works. I was scared to death to quit my job, because I had always worked. But somehow I knew I wouldn't be happy unless I did. I called my boss and told him I wasn't coming back.

Since that time I have done free-lance work at home. That's worked out pretty well, but my children are still young enough that even doing a small amount of outside work right now takes too much time from my family. Do I have any regrets? Not really. It's still a little awkward for me when I'm asked, "What do you do?" and I explain that I stay at home. I want to be proud of my decision, and down deep I am, but there's still that little voice that accuses me of not doing enough.

A pastor's wife of over forty-three years, Montelle shared her struggles with working at home, being on the job, and assisting at church:

We started out with a congregation of fifteen people, most of whom were family. Can you imagine taking on the responsibilities of pastoring a church at eighteen years of age? It has been a fun journey, even though it has had its ups and downs.

I worked in a public job all through the years, not to my liking, but I didn't have a choice if we wanted to eat. The church was so small they couldn't afford to pay us a salary. In fact, many times *we* would pay the light bill and other utility bills for the church. Many times when I was on the job, I would go into the bathroom and cry because I couldn't be home with my boys. I'd get my cry out, splash water on my face, and then go back to my typewriter. Even though I had excellent care for my children (an elderly retired couple took care of them and loved them dearly, cooking delicious meals for them), I wanted to be the one who raised them.

Now my boys are forty-two and forty-three with children of their own. They have adjusted well, and I see that they weren't damaged after all. I thank the Lord for His faithfulness to care for my children while we cared for His children.

Ronda said:

With three children, a husband to take care of, and a job to do, the only thing I'm missing is more time. I would love to do it all. I've worked full-time since I was twelve years old. Every weekend I waited tables; then throughout high school I worked summers, weekends, and evenings. Working like this all my childhood instilled a work ethic deep within me, as well as a lot of discipline. I guess it's because of all this that I take a lot of things on myself.

To be honest, I'd love to go to school full time, be with my kids full time, work full time. I just need more *me*'s to do all the things I want to do. One of my greatest weaknesses is I don't know how to rest. Even though my husband, Mike, is a high achiever, he's able to just sit down and watch an entire movie. Me, I can't sit still long enough.

I don't feel guilty about working outside the home. Being a person who needs activity and handles the demands of those activities fairly well, I don't feel panicked by working. I just need to find more ways to relax when I can. I'm learning to take whatever chances I have to relax. That may mean when I'm driving in the car, instead of listening to a teaching tape, or a work-related tape, I listen to Mozart, or a tape of Scripture readings. I'm trying to listen to soothing worship music instead of preaching tapes. I need *rest* for my spirit, not food for thought.

Dwelling on the fact that the Lord has "borne the stripes for my healing and provided all I need for eternal salvation" not only helps relax my spirit, but helps relax me physically as well.

Ilene, a single mom of two, works to provide for her family.

There are a couple of things that have helped me in dealing with the stress of working and taking care of my family without the help of a partner. I try not to compare myself with others. I know that I am limited in the amount of time I have to do all the things I need to do. If I have a choice of mopping my kitchen floor, or spending time with my son or daughter, there's no question what will wait. When I make the choice to spend time with my children rather than clean the house, that's fine, except when a friend drops by who keeps what I would consider an immaculate house. There's a lot of mental gymnastics I have to do to keep myself in balance. I really have to disregard what this friend might think, or what I think she might think, and focus on my primary goal. I want happy, healthy kids who know that if Mom could be there all the time, she would be. Being there when I can helps to demonstrate my love and priorities.

I don't have a husband around to tell me, "Don't feel guilty about this or that," so I have to rely on the voice of the Lord speaking to me, and sometimes I have to talk to myself out loud. I need to hear someone say, "That's all right; everything's going to be fine."

One day I found this note to myself scribbled on the back of an envelope in my purse: *Some people are more concerned with how their home looks than how it works. Some people are more concerned with* where *they live than* how *they live.* Wise words to keep in mind when life's responsibilities seem to be overwhelming.

As you make decisions about work and family, keep in mind that whatever path you choose, there will be advantages and disadvantages for you and your family. Examine your reasons honestly before God as to why you are choosing to work or not work outside of the home. Divide a piece of paper in half and list the pros and cons of either decision so you can see clearly what you are basing your choice on. And remember, if you're feeling a sharp pain between your eyes, it may just be that two-by-four the Lord is using to get your attention, reminding you to keep on entrusting yourself to the One who judges righteously.

Being It All, Doing It All, Losing It All

In her book *A Season at Home*, Debbie Barr talks about the myth of the working woman:

Working moms have it all: stylish clothes and haircut, briefcase, nice house, nice car, great job and happy family. . . . Supermom is immune to burnout; even after working 40–60 hours outside the home, maintaining a spotless home, having a sizzling romantic life with her husband, and spending loads of quality time with her mature, cooperative kids, she still has energy left over. . . . Underneath the myth, however, "Supermom" is very tired! Her house is not clean, her family is not deliriously happy—she's an ordinary human being with time and energy limitations.[2]

Somewhere between the myth of June Cleaver (who cleaned toilets wearing heels and pearls!) and the myth of Supermom is a real live flesh-and-blood person who loves the Lord and loves her family, but sometimes kicks the dog, yells at her kids, pretends she's already asleep when her husband comes to bed, and is rude to the telephone repairman. She doesn't mean to be so terribly human, but she is, and she's smack-dab in the middle of trying to do the hardest job of all: balancing family and career.

When that balancing act gets the better of us and we become exhausted, one of the most dangerous sacrifices we make is to our marriage relationship. In all the busyness of trying to juggle our various roles, we need to stop often and ask ourselves, "Am I taking my husband for granted?"

The Back Burner Is for Cooking, Not for Your Husband

"People watching" is one of the most enjoyable activities in which Steve and I engage. (With that admission, all of a sudden my life seems rather dull and boring!) You can learn a lot about people simply by the lost art of observation. Using this tool, we've noticed some interesting things concerning married couples. When we're sitting in a restaurant and see a couple sitting on the same side of the booth, we think the overwhelming odds are that these people are not married.

When the couple looks undistractedly into each other's eyes, holding and caressing one another with each intimate gaze, they probably are not discussing Junior's upcoming orthodontic appointment. Why is it that our relationship with our spouse is all-consuming, occupying every thought and intention—that is, until we get married? Every young married couple I know determines that they will keep the honeymoon going, but what

---

[2]Debbie Barr, *A Season at Home* (Grand Rapids, Mich.:Zondervan, 1993), pp. 18–19.

happens? Before all the rice is vacuumed out of the car, the sizzle is gone from the marriage.

Oftentimes the lack of attention toward our spouse is not motivated by a lack of love, but by a lack of planning or setting priorities. When a woman has taken on the enormous feat of working forty to sixty hours outside the home, and then comes home to work the evening shift at her *second* full-time job, is it any wonder that at some point she might run out of energy?

Too often when time and attention are doled out, the husband is left out. If he's not on the hot seat, then he's on the back burner, left to simmer and steam while work, the house, the children, band boosters, and choir rehearsal get all the attention.

Proverbs 14:1 admonishes us as women to beware: "The wise woman builds her house, but the foolish tears it down with her own hands." Of course our husband needs and deserves more time and attention. But how can we keep the love fires burning when the fuel is about used up?

Don't Waste Precious Fuel

As women who work as wage earners, in addition to being wives and mothers, it's important for us not to use up our precious reserves of time and energy by giving in to unnecessary anger. Anger can kill any thought of intimate love with a spouse. It's imperative that we divert our anger and frustrations away from those we love. When you come home from work and find the entire family sitting around in their own squalor, impatiently waiting for you to get dinner, it's not likely you will look at your husband with undefiled desire in your heart. Instead of passion taking over your body, you might have an irresistible urge to resurrect that old muzzle-loader over the fireplace. You may deal with fleeting thoughts of "crimes of passion" rather than thoughts of love.

It is understandable that a woman may be tempted to give way to anger in the face of added pressure and fatigue. Given the fact that the overwhelming reason a woman goes back to work is the need to contribute financially to the welfare of the family, it is terribly unfair for the brunt of the housework to fall entirely on her already tired shoulders. If you have a family of four, and four people made the mess, then four people should help clean it up.

One woman said, "I have too much to do at work, and when I come home at night, there is even more work waiting for me. I have a problem. When it comes time to go to bed with my husband, I want to go to sleep. The truth is, I feel numb from the neck down. Yes, I'm angry, but more than angry, I'm just plain tuckered out."

Let's face it—sometimes we do get terribly irritated with those we love. But if we get angry, are we sinning? Since we are made in the image of God, being angry is not an unreasonable reaction to things that are wrong. Throughout the centuries, God has shown *His* anger against the following: stubbornness (Exodus 4:14), idolatry (Numbers 25:3), murmuring (Numbers 11:1), lust of men (Numbers 11:33–34), pride (Numbers 12:9), disobedience (Numbers 22:22), rebellion (Numbers 32:10–13), backsliding (Deuteronomy 6:15), sin (Joshua 7:1), hypocrisy (Job 42:7), wickedness (Psalm 7:11), works of men (Jeremiah 32:30).

In Ephesians 4, words of admonishment are given which can be a great help when dealing with the difficulties of maintaining a positive marital relationship:

> Let me say this, then, speaking for the Lord: Live no longer as the unsaved do, for they are blinded and confused. Their closed hearts are full of darkness; they are far away from the life of God because they have shut their minds against him, and they cannot understand his ways. They don't care anymore about right and wrong and have given themselves over to impure ways. They stop at nothing, being driven by their evil minds and reckless lusts.
>
> But that isn't the way Christ taught you! If you have really heard his voice and learned from him the truths concerning himself, then throw off your old evil nature—the old you that was a partner in your evil ways—rotten through and through, full of lust and shame.
>
> Now your attitudes and thoughts must all be constantly changing for the better. Yes, you must be a new and different person, holy and good. Clothe yourself with this new nature.
>
> Stop lying to each other; tell the truth, for we are parts of each other and when we lie to each other we are hurting ourselves. *If you are angry, don't sin by nursing your grudge. Don't let the sun go down with you still angry—get over it quickly; for when you are angry you give a mighty foothold to the devil.* (vv. 17–27, TLB, emphasis added)

Ouch! That hurts. Read this passage again and think about the times you complained to your unsaved co-workers, and they gave you advice that was directly opposed to what the Bible says we should do. Are we opening ourselves up to counsel that encourages us to "give over to impure ways"? Are we participating in lunch-hour gossip sessions? A definition of "gossip" I find very convicting is, "Discussing a situation for which you are neither a part of the problem or a part of the solution."

I have to confess that the latter part of this scripture passage hits me between the eyes. It doesn't come naturally for me to quickly get over my hurt feelings. However, through the years I have found that the more I "nurse a grudge" against Steve, the children, or anyone, the more miserable I am.

We do need to talk to someone about our abundance of problems and scarcity of answers, but we must be sure we're talking to the right person and in the right way.

Talk Doesn't Always Come Easy

Talk to one another, but use words wisely. Nursing grudges comes as easily for me as polishing off the leftover chocolate cake. One time when Steve hurt my feelings, I was sure he had done so intentionally. All day long I mulled over what had happened. I talked to myself, feeding my feelings of rejection. I told myself, "He's right. I am a worthless person. I don't deserve to be treated in a respectful way. I don't deserve to be loved."

But did Steve say anything like this? Of course not! I had convinced myself that he had meant all the terrible things I was saying to myself, even though he had said nothing of the sort. Finally, after nursing my hurt feelings and berating myself (and after giving Steve the silent treatment for a couple of days), I opened up for conversation concerning the situation. When I told Steve why I was upset, he honestly and convincingly confessed that he had no idea what I was talking about. I had wasted a lot of time and expended a great amount of emotional energy because I had talked to myself instead of to Steve. Steve may have acted insensitively, but the additional emotional distress was my own fault because I would not talk to him. (By the way, Steve didn't even notice my "silent treatment." Since I did answer questions in a civil manner, he was unaware that I was refusing to elaborate in my usual talkative manner. To me, the silence was deafening. Men and women really *are* different!)

Sometimes we may be very angry because we assume our husband is taking deliberate advantage of us, showing total disregard for our feelings, and basically mistreating us by imposing on our good nature. At such times, it's important to *talk these things out.* However, our words should not be words of accusation, but personal confession of our feelings. Try using the "I" approach. Instead of saying to your husband, "All you think about is yourself, you are a worthless slob, and you need to help me around the house," try saying something like, "Honey, I really want to keep a house that we can all be proud of and look forward to coming home to in the evenings. I realize this may be more important to me than to anyone else in the house, but when I'm left to do it all alone, I feel devalued and unappreciated. I don't want to feel this way because it influences the way I think about you and the children. I don't want anything to distract from my love for our family."

Let me suggest that the two of you agree to make a list of things that you each need from the other. Agree together on the number of items and be specific in your suggestions. After you've written these down, sit down and talk about them together.

When you talk, *find a neutral location.* A great place to discuss things is in the car. A nice peaceful drive can be a good getaway from the phone, laundry, and kids. Hopefully, at the end of the conversation, you will be ready to stop and have a cup of coffee and find a moment to relax together. Avoid having such conversations in the bedroom. Preserve the bedroom atmosphere as a place where love and intimacy reigns. (A little side note: If you have a television in your bedroom, get rid of it. There's little time enough for each other without inviting David Letterman into the room with you.)

Keep talking. Don't think once is going to do it. Whenever things start to slip back into the old uncomfortable patterns, then talk again. Couples who plan an evening out once a week (or as often as possible) can more easily keep communicating about these "little foxes that spoil the vines" (Song of Solomon 2:15, KJV). It's not the big things that blow a marriage apart; it's the little things that eat away at the foundation of the marriage that finally topple it. Keeping the lines of communication open can help exterminate the pests that gnaw away at love.

Take turns talking. Someone has to listen. If you are the "talker" in the relationship, make a *short* statement, then sit back and patiently wait for your husband to express his feelings. Sometimes men are tagged as noncommunicative, or nontalkers, when the truth is they can't get a word in edgewise if their lives depended on it!

I am the "talker" in our marriage. I could talk the hind legs off a mule. Sometimes when I hear myself going on and on, I just want to stuff a sock in it. It takes conscious discipline on my part to talk and then shut up. There are times when I'm actually talking to myself as Steve speaks! It's amazing how much Steve will communicate when given the opportunity. He will not, however, *take* the opportunity unless I'm quiet.

Talk to the Lord together. Ecclesiastes 4:12 offers a beautiful instruction to us as married couples to draw from the unbreakable resource: "A threefold cord is not quickly broken" (RSV). We need each other for support, but the *strength* of our relationship is found in the third strand. Yes, we should talk to each other, but it's when we talk *together with God* that we are fully strengthened.

The words of the old hymn "What a Friend We Have in Jesus" are very applicable to this discussion.

O what peace we often forfeit,
O what needless pain we bear,
All because we do not carry
Everything to God in prayer.

I find it such a comfort that God has not left us as orphans to try to figure out all the intricate workings of these complicated human relationships. He is there to help us learn to love one another, if we will only call on Him for help.

My Mind Has a "Stress-Fracture"

It was a beautiful morning as I lay in bed contemplating the activities ahead. A nice leisurely Sunday morning with plenty of time for a simple breakfast, a hot cup of coffee, and a glance at the morning paper before going to church. I leaned back for one of those muscle-relaxing, terrific stretches. (I'd stretch a mile if I didn't have to walk back.) As I let go for a generous stretch, it happened. Right in the middle of stretching, my back went out! Oh, dread!

I could hardly make it through the day. I kept thinking I'd get better, but as the days went by, my neck became even more immobile. In order to drive I had to move my entire torso to see out the window. Finally, I submitted to the pain and made my way to the chiropractor.

After a series of adjustments to my miserably inflamed neck and back, he asked me a question: "Do you have any stress in your life?" What a stupid question! Do you know anyone who doesn't have stress in her life?

Stress had become so woven into the fiber of my being, I had actually trained myself to depend on stress to get things done. After abusing myself in this manner, was it any wonder that the doctor told me he could adjust my back every day, but because my muscles were so tightly knotted, they would pull my back out of position again. My real problem was *stress*.

Is it the will of God that our lives be dominated with stress and fatigue? I don't believe so. When I'm feeling strung out on stress, I should recognize the warning signal that I'm off track and need to get my priorities back in God's order. It's my only hope of sanity.

Isaiah 26:3 gives us the promise, "Thou wilt keep him in perfect peace, whose mind is stayed on thee: because he trusteth in thee" (KJV). Verse 4 goes on to say, "Trust ye in the Lord forever: for in the Lord Jehovah is *everlasting strength*" (emphasis added). What a wonderful promise to mankind throughout the generations! We are not the only people in history for whom life has been stressful. Admittedly, some of our stress is self-induced because we have extended ourselves financially, buying things we don't need with money we don't have. On the other hand, many experience stress because of legitimate hardships: a terribly ill child, a troubled marriage, a death in the family, lost employment, or the demands of taking care of elderly parents. Regardless of the circumstances, peace is to be had when we exchange our worries and endless activities for trust and direction from God.

Mike and Nancy had only been married for eight months when Mike was injured on the job. The fall from the roof on which he was working left him a quadriplegic. Any progress they could expect would only come with great difficulty and minimal rewards. Visiting with him and his family, I was amazed. With no insurance or visible means of support, this couple had placed themselves right in the middle of God's capable hands. The faith they displayed in the face of tremendous disappointment and heartache was a testimony that "the peace of God, which surpasses all comprehension" *really can* "guard your hearts and your minds in Christ Jesus" (Philippians 4:7).

Humanly speaking, this was the most stressful of situations, yet God's peace reigned supremely in that hospital room. The difficult three months that preceded my visit had served to refine this couple as pure gold. I've lived long enough to know that hard times don't make us bitter or better, but the choices we make do. Choosing *peace* rather than *panic* is the way to go. Such peace is only found in a sincere, childlike trust in God.

Romans 8:6 shows us the way out of stress and into peace and reveals the danger of being overly involved with the things of the flesh. "For to be carnally minded is death; but to be spiritually minded is life and peace" (KJV). Also, 2 Corinthians 13:11 tells us to "Be happy. Grow in Christ. Pay attention to what I have said. Live in harmony and peace. And may the God of love and peace be with you" (TLB). We need not surrender our lives to turmoil.

Perhaps the words of this old familiar hymn will reinforce your confidence in God's ability to meet all needs.

> Be not dismayed whate'er betide; God will take care of you.
> Beneath His wings of love abide; God will take care of you.
>
> Thro' days of toil when heart doth fail; God will take care
> of you.
> When dangers fierce your path assail; God will take care
> of you.
>
> All you may need He will provide; God will take care of you.
> Nothing you ask will be denied; God will take care of you.
>
> No matter what may be the test; God will take care of you.
> Lean, weary one, upon His breast; God will take care of you.
>
> God will take care of you, through every day, o'er all
> the way.
> He will take care of you, God will take care of you.[3]

---

[3]Civilla D. Martin and W. Stillman Martin.

6

Stop the World:
I Want to Get Off!

As we fix lunches, drive car pools, make cookies for Sunday school class, sing in the choir, help our children with their homework, pay our taxes, and pray for our pastors, what does all the "political stuff" have to do with our lives? What does it matter if Washington, D.C. is power gone amok? Do we care that our country is also *running on empty with no exit in sight*?

The question posed to us Christian women is one we dare not ignore. It has echoed down the corridors of time and now rings in our ears. Lamentations 1:12 asks us as we serve in our family rooms and in the boardrooms of America, "Is it nothing to all you who pass this way?" In other words, "What does this have to do with *my* life?"

I propose that the state of affairs this country is in, and where it is ultimately going, has *plenty* to do with our lives as everyday, all-day-long women. Time is running out. If we really do want our children to be able to grow up in a country where they will enjoy the benefits of freedom of religion, speech, thought, and action—the way we've been blessed—then we must first open our eyes and take a good hard look at the situation. Things are bad. Perhaps they are even worse than we think. Perhaps it's too late for our children. I sincerely hope not!

In Pat Robertson's book *The Turning Tide*, he says, "One of the oldest truisms of historians is the idea that when the women of any culture no longer stand for virtue and moral restraints, that culture is doomed to collapse. That is clearly a risk we face today in this country."[1]

Christian women, I challenge you to stand up to the task at hand. "Sons of righteous kings were not necessarily righteous. Sons of wicked kings were not necessarily wicked. The key ingredient in shaping the religious faith of the king was the king's mother. That is why the mothers are very carefully listed. It seems clear to me that the order is simple in the pages of holy history: Mothers shaped kings—kings shape nations—and God blesses or curses nations depending on how they respond to Him. . . . It seldom happens that a people will arise above their leaders in faith and morality. If the leaders are corrupt, the nation will sooner or later be corrupt. Good leaders can lift and inspire people, but seldom, over the long run, will people continuously achieve any lofty standards beyond those set by their leaders.[2]

The old saying "The hand that rocks the cradle rules the world" is still true. Without godly mothers raising godly children, then we will be left either with no leaders, or with leaders who have no concept or capacity to communicate godly values.

My People Have Forgotten Me!

Consider the sobering parallel between God's relationship with the nation of Israel and His concern for His people in America. In the history of God's dealings with Israel, His love is evident. However, Israel's behavior had a direct bearing on God's blessing. In the book of Jeremiah, chapter eighteen, God says, "At another moment I might speak concerning a nation or concerning a kingdom to build up or to plant it, if it does evil in My sight by not obeying My voice, then I will think better of the good with which I had promised to bless it. . . . Thus says the Lord: 'Behold, I am fashioning calamity against you and devising a plan against you. Oh turn back, each of you from his evil

[1]Pat Robertson, *The Turning Tide* (Dallas, Tex.: Word Publishing, 1993), p. 170.
[2]Ibid., p. 170.

way, and reform your ways and your deeds' " (vv. 9–11).

Israel responded, "It's hopeless! For we are going to follow our own plans, and each of us will act according to the stubbornness of his evil heart" (v. 12).

God's response continues: "For My people have forgotten Me; they burn incense to worthless gods and they have stumbled from their ways, from the ancient paths, to walk in bypaths, not on a highway, to make their land a desolation, an object of perpetual hissing; everyone who passes by it will be astonished and shake his head" (vv. 15–16).

Then Israel said, "Come and let us devise plans against Jeremiah. Surely the law is not going to be lost to the priest, nor counsel to the sage, nor the divine word to the prophet! Come on and let us strike at him with our tongue, and let us give no heed to any of his words" (v. 18).

The people of Israel were depending on the historical connection of righteousness (the priesthood, and the divine word of the prophets) to exempt them from the promise of doom if repentance did not take place.

We Americans should not be equally foolish to assume God is obligated to save us just because our nation was once built on stones of righteousness and the blood of godly men. Other countries have fallen, and we too will fall if we do not repent as a nation and turn from the evil path we are barreling down at this point in history.

This thought-provoking quotation is from Sir Alex Faser Tytler (1742–1813), a Scottish jurist and historian who was widely known in his day. He was a professor of Universal History at Edinburgh University. The following quotation is from the 1801 collection of his lectures.

> A democracy cannot exist as a permanent form of government. It can only exist until the voters discover that they can vote themselves largess from the public treasury. From that time on, the majority always votes for the candidates promising the most benefits from the public treasury, with the result that a democracy always collapses over loose fiscal policy, always followed by a dictatorship.
>
> The average age of the world's great civilizations has been two hundred years. These nations have progressed through this sequence:

From bondage to spiritual faith;
from spiritual faith to great courage;
from great courage to liberty;
from liberty to abundance;
from abundance to selfishness;
from selfishness to complacency;
from complacency to apathy;
from apathy to dependency;
from dependency back again into bondage.

"From Spiritual Faith to Great Courage"

Now, consider the words of two of the great men who gave their lives and fortunes to establish this nation:

George Washington said, "Reason and experience forbid us to expect public morality in the absence of religious principle." He also said, "It is impossible to govern rightly without God and the Bible."

John Quincy Adams, sixth President of the United States, said, "The highest glory of the American Revolution was this: It connected, in one indissoluble bond, the principle of civil government with the principle of Christianity." He also said, "We have not a government strong enough to restrain the unbridled passions of men. This constitution was made only for a religious people. It is wholly inadequate for any other."

How far have we strayed as a people from the concepts found in the words of these great leaders? That dangerous distance from then to now is visible in the following areas of our lives.

Education

Even though we have heard it many times, the following quote leaves us unsettled: "In 1940, teachers identified the top problems in American schools as: talking out of turn, chewing gum, making noise and running in the hall. In 1990, teachers listed drugs, alcohol, pregnancy, suicide, rape and assault."[3]

With the falling SAT scores and the new emphasis in recent years to use the public school system to introduce our children to condoms and "political correctness," no wonder the educa-

---

[3]William Bennett, "What Really Ails America," *Reader's Digest* (April 1994), p. 197.

tion system has strayed so far from its intended beginning. Listen to what the founding father of education, Noah Webster, said: "In my view, the Christian religion is the most important one of the first things in which all children, under a free government, ought to be instructed. . . . No truth is more evident to my mind than that the Christian religion must be the basis of any government intended to secure the rights and privileges of a free people."

In public schools, our children are actually being "untaught" some important truths and are also being taught some very destructive behavior. History has been reworked to fit the evil agenda of those who would deny our Christian heritage and the intent of our Founding Fathers. While the Ten Commandments are being stripped from the walls of our public schools, books like *Heather Has Two Mommies* and *Daddy's Roommate* are being added to the library shelves.

The Media

Our hearts and minds are constantly being shaped and reshaped by many influences. Even the seemingly innocuous act of turning on the evening news exposes us to a world view that runs counter to what we as Christians hold dear. If we are not *discerning* in what we watch and hear, we run the risk of being swayed by the subtle manipulations of a powerful group. Who are these people who tell us what is important and determine what is worthy of our viewing?

The "media elite," those individuals who are in charge of dispensing the news, are not as neutral and unbiased as they would have us believe. When over 60,000 men met in 1994 at the Hoosier Dome in Indianapolis for the midwest convention of The Promise Keepers, a pro-family, pro-Christian values organization of men, it was hard to find any mention of it in the national newspapers or television coverage.

A few years ago, I was in the habit of reading *U.S.A. Today*. This national newspaper provided a way to quickly find out what was happening across the country. On one particular day, the paper had given the full front page to the pro-abortion rally held in Washington that weekend. Even though I didn't enjoy seeing the "splash" and obvious support for abortion, I understood that this was news and worth reporting whether or not I agreed with the rally.

A few weeks after the pro-abortion rally, the March for Life, supporting the life and protection of the unborn, took place in Washington, D.C. Excitedly, I picked up *U.S.A. Today* to see what they had to say. My excitement was short-lived, for their coverage of the gathering of hundreds of thousands of people consisted of a tiny picture of the pro-life marchers. The real coverage was given to a small group of people who were *protesting* the march. The difference in coverage was so obviously biased that I immediately wrote the editor of the newspaper and told him I would never, ever buy it again. I felt the paper was little more than a propaganda machine for abortion. As far as I can tell, nothing has changed in their unbalanced coverage. I continue to find my news information elsewhere.

It should not be a surprise that this and other newspapers, news magazines, networks, and cable news programs are unfair and biased. The frustrating part is that they *talk* neutrality, but they are not neutral at all. Who are the people who control the media?

- 50% list no religious affiliation.
- 86% never go to church.
- 90% favor abortion rights.
- 97% think the government should not regulate sex.
- Only 25% think homosexuality is wrong.
- 54% see nothing wrong with adultery.

Secular television officials, who are largely biased against Christianity and its moral guidelines, admit that they are not in it for the money. They are trying to move their viewers toward their own ideal of the good society.[4]

Sometimes the bias against our Christian values is not even disguised as neutrality. Many times the antireligious message gets quite brazen. While reading the Sunday newspaper one afternoon, I turned to the comics for a little humor and levity. Garry Trudeau's *Doonesbury* was working overtime to reinforce, as well as reshape, the attitudes of his readers. In the cartoon, the mom and dad were discussing the fact that perhaps it was time for them to introduce their son to the discipline of going to

---

[4]Robertson, op. cit. pp. 131–132.

church. As the parents discussed the idea with their child, they explained that even though the child probably would not enjoy going to church, it was something he should experience. The child asked if church was going to be boring. The father explained that when he was a kid he hated going to church, but his parents made him go, and so the child must endure it as well. "You have to put in pew times, like Mom and I did."

The child then asked, "What if I like it?" The parents obviously had never even considered the possibility of him liking church. "Like it? What do you mean?" the father said. The mother, dismissing even the possibility, said, "We'll cross that bridge when we get there, honey."

I thought cartoons were supposed to be funny. Isn't that why they are referred to as the "funnies"? It seems every time there is a remote opportunity, the media puts in another dig against all that is good and wholesome.

Entertainment

Television

The TV is my shepherd. My spiritual growth shall want. It maketh me to sit down and do nothing for His name's sake because it requireth all my spare time. It keepeth me from doing my duty as a Christian because it presenteth so many good shows that I must see.

It restoreth my knowledge of the things of the world and keepeth me from the study of God's Word. It leadeth me in the paths of failing to attend the evening church services and doing nothing for the kingdom of God. Yet, though I shall live to be a hundred, I shall keep viewing my TV as long as it will work, for it is my closest friend. Its sounds and its picture they comfort me.

It presenteth entertainment before me and keepeth me from doing important things with my family. It fills my head with ideas which differ from those in the Word of God.

Surely no good thing will come of my life because of so many wasted hours, and I shall dwell in my remorse and regrets forever.[5]

Perhaps no part of society is more openly hostile and ulti-

---

[5]Author unknown.

mately destructive to the godly values we cherish than the entertainment industry. In an article for *Christianity Today*, Lloyd Billingsley observed, "I cannot remember any episode of any show in which a character was religiously motivated to do or not to do some important act. . . . In the unwritten constitution of television, the separation of church and screen is strictly adhered to, even in family programs such as *The Cosby Show*. God is effectively written out of existence (except in repeated ejaculations like 'Oh my God!'), and Judeo-Christian values on such things as adultery and divorce are disregarded.

"In 1990 the Fox Television Network chose to promote its most popular show with a satirical scene that mocked a family saying grace. With all of the Simpsons gathered around their dinner table, Bart solemnly intones, 'Dear God, we pay for all this stuff ourselves, so thanks for nothing.' "[6]

Movies

As Christian women we must keep our eyes open. The movie industry knows what it is doing. Even though the majority of those in control of what we see and hear are not Christian, or even tolerant to the Christian message, they are "spiritual" people. Understanding the thirst this society has for meaning and spirituality, they have served up quite a feast for us. Lloyd Billingsley says, "This is a group that seldom questions the magical healing powers of crystals, where stars pay handsome fees to learn esoteric systems of Eastern meditation or to liberate their own 'inner child,' and the ability of certain enlightened guides to 'channel' for long-dead souls is accepted without embarrassment. It is, in short, a community in which Shirley MacLaine has more followers than either Jesus or Moses."[7] Moviemakers are "evangelists" with a bully pulpit to which we, the church, too often pay our tithes and offerings.

Music

There is a whole new type of music that has captured the attention of our young people. The basis of this music is violence and anger. One of the peddlers of this message is a man named

[6]Lloyd Billingsley, "Hollywood vs. America," *Christianity Today* (1985), p. 79.
[7]Ibid., p. 84.

Tupac Shakur. You may not have heard of him, but millions of young people have, and millions have bought his CD's. He was wanted in Atlanta for allegedly shooting two off-duty police officers, and he was wanted in New York for allegedly raping a woman in his hotel suite. He was also wanted in Los Angeles for allegedly beating up a limo driver on the Fox lot.

Is this kind of behavior the exception? Too many other entertainers have just as checkered a past and present. Even while these singers and actors are selling a million CD's, their lives continue to go downhill. Shakur said of his own life in the April 1994 issue of *Entertainment Weekly*, "I live in hell. I have no friends. I never sleep; I can never close my eyes. Can you imagine what it's like to be who I am?" Yet there are countless young people who would love to be in his shoes. The music industry has given these troubled people a platform to share their anger and, by elevating them to the status of celebrity, has created very questionable role models for our youth.

"On television, indecent exposure is celebrated by all ages as a virtue. There was a time when personal failures, subliminal desires, and perverse tastes were accompanied by guilt, or at least silence. Today they are tickets to appear as guests on talk shows. . . . People are losing their capacity for shock, disgust and outrage. This is not a good thing to get used to."[8]

These Are the Stones

We desperately need to come back to the foundation stones on which this nation was built.

> These are the stones in the foundation,
> And they were laid many years ago;
> And on these stones was built a mighty nation;
> Take them away and down it goes.
>
> There is a God and in Him we trust;
> His Word is true and His ways are just;
> In His hand is the heart of the King;
> We ask Him before we do anything.
>
> When fires of lust are never quenched,
> Death is the final consequence;

---

[8]Bennett, op. cit.

Heaven's real and hell is hot;
Right is right and wrong is not.

There is a God, in Him we trust;
His Word is true and His ways are just;
And when all is said and done,
He'll want to know what we did with His Son.[9]

Are We Part of the Problem, or Part of the Solution?

With all our work and family responsibilities weighing us down, it's difficult to get involved in politics or social problems. There are Christian women who feel that it's not their place to worry about these things. I can understand the aversion to becoming entangled with the pressing issues of the day. Some may feel that there really isn't much we can do, and that the political process has become next to useless. It is true that our political system cannot deliver perfectly what it promises, yet we still have the freedom in this country to make known our views publicly. We do have a voice in who governs and in how they govern, but only if we speak up! Our freedom to participate in government *will* be taken from us if we fail to exercise this responsibility. As we watch other nations reeling from wars that are destroying such freedoms, we need to guard against complacency. What makes any of us think this couldn't happen to us? We are accountable to God—who has placed us in this country with its many freedoms—to keep in touch with what is happening and to fight the flood of evil. *Ignorance is no excuse, for if we are not part of the solution, then we are part of the problem.* Perhaps the following information will help persuade those of us who are busy, but not too busy, to be involved.

The following statistics were compiled by the research foundation of the liberal Children's Defense Fund. They illustrate the moral decline in American youth. *Every day* the following events happen:

- 2,795 teenage girls get pregnant, a 500% increase since 1966.

---

[9]Words and music by Steve and Annie Chapman, as recorded on *Waiting to Hear* CD (Times and Seasons Music, Inc., BMI, 1993). Used by permission.

- 1,106 teenage girls have abortions, a 1,100% increase since 1966.
- 4,219 teenagers contract a sexually transmitted disease, a 335% increase since 1966.
- 135,000 children bring a gun or other weapon to school.
- 10 children are killed by guns.
- 6 teenagers commit suicide, a 300% increase since 1966.
- 211 children are convicted of drug use.

"What these statistics show," according to Pat Robertson, "is that, despite our vast wealth, affluence, and international status, this nation is hardly better off than the most deprived Third World countries when it comes to the emotional well-being of our children. But even more, the most serious deprivation is not a matter of food, shelter, or material comforts, but a raging famine in the human heart."[10]

The Center for Disease Control and Prevention reported in 1994 on teens, sex, and disease:[11]

- 72% of all high school seniors have had sexual intercourse.
- 19% of all high school seniors have had at least four sexual partners.
- 1,415 AIDS cases have been reported in teenagers ages 13–19.
- 12,712 AIDS cases have been reported in young people ages 20–24, many of those probably infected during adolescence.
- 3 million teens have sexually transmitted diseases, including gonorrhea, herpes, and hepatitis B.
- AIDS is the sixth leading cause of death among young people ages 15–24.

We've come a long way with all our freedom and liberation. In fact, we may have gone all the way!

As responsible mothers, we need to be informed. The survival of our families may depend on this knowledge. Is there any hope for this country? The immoral path we have chosen as a nation will ultimately lead to our demise if we continue on it. And even now, this moral downslide is affecting our way of life in more immediate ways. There was a time when we could

---

[10]Robertson, op. cit. p. 192.
[11]*The Tennessean* (April 2, 1994).

safely walk down the street after dark. Now, even in the safest of communities, the wisdom of being outside, or even at the mall, in the evenings is questionable.

What Should We Do?

Steve and I were honored to sing at the dedication ceremony of the Focus on the Family facilities in Colorado Springs, Colorado, in September 1993. Charles Colson was the keynote speaker that day. He made a statement that all America should hear: "We are witnessing in America the most terrifying thing that could happen to a society—the death of conscience."

As infuriating as it is to live in a nation that has endorsed evil and shunned good, nonetheless, we as Christians need to look at ourselves first. The nation's most severe problems are found within the hearts of American families. *The answers to the problems that plague our country are found not in the White House, but in our house.* Moms and dads, we must *start at home* to create and maintain a godly, secure environment for our children—a strong shelter from the evils they will face in the world.

Our son, Nathan, went on a retreat with the youth leaders of our church. During the evening they were each called on to share their life story. Nathan was the only one, in a group of seven youth workers, whose father had stayed with the family.

Where is conscience formed and reinforced? A knowledge of right and wrong is established in the home. Let your children know where you stand on issues of morality and teach them to be involved in the larger community as well. Even if your contributions cannot be huge, let your children learn early that Christians *can* make a difference in our world, and that we must never allow ourselves to think we are too insignificant to make any real difference. We must start reclaiming our godly heritage in our homes.

Put Your Money Where Your Values Are

What if God's people really took their own cause seriously and put their money where their values are? Think of the increased good that wonderful organizations such as Focus on the Family, American Family Association, Right-to-Life, Coalition Against Pornography, the many local Crisis Pregnancy Centers, and other groups could do if much more money was given and more time volunteered. If you have any question as to what is important to you, then take a look at the check stubs in your checkbook and examine where the majority of your resources are going. That's where your treasure lies. We are warned to be careful where we place our monetary efforts: "Do not lay up for yourselves treasures upon earth, where moth and rust destroy, and where thieves break in and steal. But lay up for yourselves treasures in heaven, where neither moth nor rust destroys, and where thieves do not break in or steal; for where your treasure is, there will your heart be also" (Matthew 6:19–21). The best way to fight greed is to give our money away.

Teach your children early to set aside a portion of their allowance for giving to others, or help them find ways to make some money for contributing to a worthwhile project. Choose a project to focus on as a family: supporting a missionary, "adopting" an impoverished family or child, giving to help promote a particular political candidate. Decorate a bulletin board together and keep it in a prominent place to show your children how their money is helping to make a difference.

Put Your Time Where Your Values Are

Time is one of our most sought-after commodities. Twenty-four hours in a day simply doesn't seem to be enough for any of us. I asked a friend if she could have anything in the world, what would she want? Without hesitation she said, "Time!"

We all agree that we have too much to do and not enough time to do it all. And yet our country needs us, as citizens and Christians, to help turn the tide of immorality and ungodliness. So what are we to do? The truth is, most of us *do* find time for the things we consider important. As we look at how we're spending our valuable resource of time, we need to be willing to consider that God might have us be more involved in volunteer work—be it political, social, or through our churches. The benefits of such involvement can reach not only to those outside our families, but to us and our children as well. Our children are probably not aware of the money we send to various organizations or put in the offering plate at church. But taking them to a soup kitchen once a month to help serve the homeless could change their whole outlook on life. And we can be helped, too, by glimpsing the bigger picture and not letting ourselves be isolated in our homes, seeing only the unending daily chores which can easily lead to discouragement.

Perhaps your present responsibilities will not permit you to run for public office, but there are things you *can* do that require minimal time and yet can accomplish a great amount of good.

1. *Spend five minutes a day in prayer for this country and its leaders.* Perhaps you could do this as a family after your evening meal. First Timothy 2 says, "I exhort therefore, that, first of all, supplications, prayers, intercessions, and giving of thanks, be made for all men; for kings, and for all that are in authority; that we may lead a quiet and peaceable life in all godliness and honesty. For this is good and acceptable in the sight of God our Savior; who will have all men to be saved, and to come unto the knowledge of the truth" (vv. 1–4, KJV).

What is the right way to pray for those leaders who seem to be in opposition to what is godly? I can't imagine the apostle Paul praying that God would bless Nero and give him the strength to persecute and kill even more Christians. In the same way, I can't bring myself to pray that God will bless and help a president who passes legislation against the unborn and promotes lifestyles destructive to individuals, as well as to our society as a whole.

How, then, should we pray for such leaders?

Pray that they will be saved. "The Lord is not slack concerning his promise, as some men count slackness; but is longsuffering to us ward, not willing that any should perish, but that all should come to repentance" (2 Peter 3:9, KJV).

Pray that they will come to the knowledge of the truth. "And the Spirit and the bride say, Come. And let him that heareth say, Come. And let him that is athirst come. And whosoever will, let him take the water of life freely" (Revelation 22:17, KJV).

2. *Write to those in leadership and encourage them to do what is right.* Encourage your school-age children to compose their own letters. "Another reason for right living is this: you know how late it is; time is running out. Wake up, for the coming of the Lord is nearer now than when we first believed. The night is far gone, the day of his return will soon be here. So quit the evil deeds of darkness and put on the armor of right living, as we who live in the daylight should! Be decent and true in everything

you do so that all can approve your behavior. Don't spend your time in wild parties and getting drunk or in adultery and lust, or fighting, or jealousy. But ask the Lord Jesus Christ to help you live as you should, and don't make plans to enjoy evil" (Romans 13:11–14, TLB).

3. *Get involved personally in the election process.* You may not be able to do all of the things listed below, but choose what will work for you and your family.

- Go to school board meetings.
- Vote in both primary and general elections.
- Take time to watch political debates on television.
- Go to community meetings where you can meet and confront the candidates.
- Financially support those candidates who are in agreement with you on important issues.
- Give time to a candidate. Answer the phone, send out mailings, pass out flyers.
- Encourage your church to get involved. During the last primary election our church passed out a "score card" for each of the candidates. This told the public where each candidate stood on the key issues. Steve and I took the card into the booth with us. It felt good to be informed, instead of voting for the friendliest face or the most recognizable name.
- Talk to your children about the candidates you are supporting and why.
- Be willing to be a fool for Christ's sake. Take a stand. Open your mouth. Be counted.

Time Is Running Out

I am convinced, without reservation, that Christ's return is imminent, even though we can't know the exact day or time. (Those who insist on trying to pinpoint this event should read Matthew 24!) When Steve and I talk about the soon return of Christ, I automatically start to think about our children. When they were small we concentrated on the fact that Jesus was going to come to take care of us. This is true. Praise the Lord!

But what should we be teaching our children now that they are older? Not only is it important that they be taught to live for

Christ, but, in these days, they must also be taught to be willing to die for Christ.

As busy women consumed with the needs of our families, we may feel overwhelmed at the thought of keeping informed as to what is happening in our society. But we are not solitary islands; we are part of a community family. What is happening around us does affect our families. We are living in a country that has turned its back on God and on the godly values on which it was built. However, we mustn't throw up our hands and surrender to the forces around us. The future of our children and their children hangs in the balance. In our efforts to do what is right for our own, let us keep our eyes open and our hearts ready to hear His voice, and to make our hands and feet available for His service wherever He calls.

I realize that pointing out the need for social responsibility and action can be fuel for the flames of overcommitment. There are women who find it more fulfilling to picket the local abortion clinic than to fix dinner for their families. Often this imbalanced drive may be motivated by a latent guilt. An examination of the motives of the heart would be important for this particular woman so that a balance may be achieved between home and community involvement.

It may seem impossible to be concerned about the actions of Congress or the moral decline in our schools when you're not sure your newborn is going to survive the vigorous attention and embraces of his older siblings. But we must see that our responsibilities *do* extend beyond our own four walls. Our nation is *running on empty*, and we need to open our eyes and open our hearts to hear God's voice of instruction on how to help our country in its hour of need.

One day when absolutely disgusted with the situation in our country, Steve and I seriously talked about heading for the hills. We wanted to take our children and go live in a log cabin somewhere in the mountains of West Virginia. We decided we could home-school our children, I could grow a garden, and Steve could hunt. (Well, okay, I could grow a BIG garden.) We could quit fighting this seemingly impossible "culture war." In the middle of our plans born in desperation, we realized there were two very good reasons we couldn't give up the fight. Those two reasons were Nathan and Heidi.

I'm Going to Leave This World Someday[12]

I used to be content just to think about heaven,
But lately in my children's eyes, I see the reflection
Of a world that's growing darker with every passing day;
It's the world I'm going to leave them when I leave this place.

I know I'm going to leave this world someday;
It is the hope of every pilgrim;
But I've gotta change this world somehow,
 make it a better place,
'Cause I know I'm gonna leave this world to my children.

I want to see the light of heaven
 shining in my children's eyes,
So I'm going to fight the darkness until the day I die.

---

[12]Words and music by Steve and Annie Chapman, as recorded on *No Regrets* CD
(Times and Seasons Music, Inc., BMI, 1989). Used by permission.

7

Me Forgive? Forget It!

Every saint has a past, and every sinner has a future.

Recently, we had dinner with our friends Ken and Kathy. Although we have stayed close through the years, our busy schedules have kept us from getting together as often as we'd like.

We eagerly began our cram course in "Hey, what's been happening with you two?" It didn't take long before the conversation became brutally honest. There was a problem, a really big problem: They had a rebellious, wayward son. We were witnessing a parent's worst nightmare. Can there be anything more hurtful to parents than seeing their child out of control and on a path of self-destruction? The bloody trail of broken dreams, hurt feelings, and utter despair were being discussed without any attempt at hiding their feelings. After hearing the painful accounting of the latest in late-night escapades and bad choices, I asked Ken and Kathy a simple question, "What's all this stress doing to the two of you?"

They answered very matter-of-factly, "We hate each other and we want a divorce. We are falling apart!"

For the next three hours we talked and prayed. Here was a home on the precipice, with fragile lives on the brink. As the evening unfolded, the underlying anger and repressed rage thickened the air. For nearly two decades these two lovely peo-

ple had terrorized each other with their civilized hostility. It
became obvious that this mom and dad bore at least some of the
responsibility for their son's willful behavior.

Ken and Kathy continued to discuss the situation between
them, with Steve and me serving as mediators. The different
way in which each of them dealt with their conflicts was re-
vealing. Kathy wanted to relate entirely on a soul level. She
wanted to talk about all the hurts of the past years. Over and
over she kept coming back to situations where she felt degraded
and put down. She remembered every indignity, every insensitive comment Ken had made. She had a very extensive accounting system of wrongs committed.

On the other hand, Ken wanted to relate on a spiritual level.
He readily admitted he had made mistakes, but what may have
been a sincere attempt to apply the scriptural principle of "forgetting things in the past and pressing on toward Christ" did
not sit well with Kathy. She didn't want to hear Bible verses
quoted or hymns sung. She wanted to hear, "Yes, I treated you
disrespectfully in front of the children. Yes, I have sided with
my mother when I should have taken up for you." She needed
to hear, "Kathy, I was very, very wrong." But most of all she
needed to hear Ken say, "Will you forgive me?"

After a bit of prodding, Ken finally turned to Kathy and said,
"I was wrong. Will you forgive me?"

Kathy sat and stared—cold and stoned-faced—at Ken. After
a painful silence she said, "You don't mean it. Anyway the only
reason you asked for forgiveness was because you were told to."
She continued on, choking back the tears. "How can I forgive
you after all that's happened? It's gone on for so long; I think it's
too late."

Oh, how sad! What poverty of spirit we demonstrate! Why
do we go on hurting one another and stubbornly withhold our
forgiveness? There is only one hope for this couple, just as there
is only one hope for all families. That one hope for reconciliation
and restoration is to *forgive*. Unforgiveness consumes so much
of the fuel that powers our lives. Even our physical movement
is hindered by unforgiveness. "Unconfessed sin causes the very
bones to waste away" (Psalm 32:3, NIV). But how do we forgive
a spouse for marital unfaithfulness? How do we forgive unkind,
cutting comments, and the basic devaluing of one another that
tears people apart? Hopefully, the following will help us to see
not only the importance of forgiving, but also *how to forgive*.

Forgive As Christ Forgave

What would we have done if when we came to God in desperate need of forgiveness, He had said, "Look, you should have come to me years ago. You have totally messed up your life and the lives of those you supposedly love. You've broken my commandments. You've gone too far; you've done too many bad things. It's simply too late. Sorry!"

Of course this never happened; nor will it ever happen. Romans 5 offers us words of hope that have consoled the heart of every hardened sinner throughout time, myself being one of them.

Christ forgave while we were sinners.

"You see, at just the right time, when we were still powerless, Christ died for the ungodly. Very rarely will anyone die for a righteous man, though for a good man someone might possibly dare to die. But God demonstrates his own love for us in this: While we were still sinners, Christ died for us" (vv. 6–8, NIV). These are powerful words. God sent Jesus to die for us, not because we were good, but because He loved us.

Never has there been a more wonderful message of healing, hope, love, and salvation. God did not turn us away when we came pleading for forgiveness. In like manner, we should not turn our fellow strugglers away when they ask for *our* forgiveness.

Which one of us doesn't need a second chance (or even better, seventy times seven chances) in our life? In the American Family Association newsletter, Dr. Donald Wildmon, President of AFA, shared a beautiful story about forgiveness. He recounted an incident that happened while Dr. A.J. Cronin, a physician from England, was practicing medicine. A young nurse was put in charge of a little boy who was brought into the hospital with complications from diphtheria. The boy's throat was choked with phlegm, and he was not given much chance of survival. His breathing tube had to be cleaned out regularly to keep the breathing passage clear.

As the young nurse sat with the child through the night, she carelessly fell asleep. When she awakened she found the tube blocked and the boy gasping for air. Instead of following the logical procedure of clearing the tube, she panicked and ran out of the room to find the doctor. By the time the nurse and Dr. Cronin got back, the boy was dead.

Dr. Cronin was furious with the nurse for her irresponsibility and promptly wrote a recommendation to the board to revoke her credentials. The nurse stood before the very angry doctor as he read the letter of dismissal. "Well, have you nothing to say for yourself?" asked Dr. Cronin in a harsh voice. There was silence, and then came the stammering plea, "Give me . . . give me another chance."

Shocked at even the request for mercy, Dr. Cronin refused to change his mind. There was no question; this was an unforgivable mistake. Her negligence had cost this boy his life. Her punishment was set. But throughout that night as he tried to sleep, all he could hear were words that came from deep in his soul: "Forgive us our trespasses. . . ."

The next morning Dr. Cronin went to his desk, tore up the report, and extended mercy to one who did not deserve it but who had humbly requested a second chance. As it turned out this young nurse became the head nurse of a large hospital and was one of the most honored nurses in all of England.

Which one of us has lived in such a way as to have never stood pleading for a second chance? Because of Christ's sacrifice on the cross, we are all eligible for that mercy. Can we do less to one another than to forgive as Christ forgave?

Christ forgave before we even asked for forgiveness.

In our helpless state of depravity Christ provided the means for our forgiveness. We didn't deserve this provision; in fact, He did all this before we even knew our need of Him, for we were spiritually dead in our sins. Ephesians 2:4–5 and 8 says, "But because of his great love for us, God who is rich in mercy, made us alive with Christ even when we were dead in transgressions . . . it is by grace you have been saved . . . it is *the* gift of God" (NIV, emphasis added).

Christ forgave out of compassion.

First Corinthians 5 speaks of an immoral man who was punished by the church. This punishment had brought him to repentance, but the people of the church were not willing to forgive him and receive him back. Second Corinthians 2 reveals the very heart of forgiveness as Paul, referring to this incident, spoke of correcting the evil in their midst: "If anyone has caused grief, he has not so much grieved me as he has grieved all of you, to some extent—not to put it too severely. The punishment inflicted on him by the majority is sufficient for him. Now instead, you ought to forgive and comfort him, so that he will not be overwhelmed by excessive sorrow. I urge you, therefore, to reaffirm your love for him. . . . If you forgive anyone, I also forgive him. And what I have forgiven—if there was anything to forgive—I have forgiven in the sight of Christ for your sake, *in order that Satan might not outwit us. For we are not unaware of his schemes*" (vv. 5–8, 10–11, NIV, emphasis added).

Most of the ground that Satan gains in the lives of Christians is due to unforgiveness. We are warned to forgive others so that Satan cannot take advantage of us. Why is forgiveness so critical to our freedom? Because of the cross. God didn't give us what we deserve; He gave us what we needed according to His mercy. We are to be merciful just as our heavenly Father is merciful (Luke 6:36). We are to forgive as we have been forgiven. Ephesians 4:31–32 reminds us to "get rid of all *bitterness, rage* and *anger, brawling* and *slander,* along with every form of *malice.* Be *kind* and *compassionate* to one another, *forgiving* each other, just as in Christ God *forgave* you" (NIV, emphasis added). The first part of this scripture text contains many words that we, as human beings, naturally feel when we have been wronged. However, the freedom from these emotions can only be experienced after we have dealt with these feelings and have forgiven others, even as we too have been forgiven. Christ does not forgive us *because* we forgive others; however, having received forgiveness from God, we are then *able* to pass it on to others.

Is forgiving the same as forgetting? I don't believe so. Psalm 103:12 says "as far as the east is from the west, so far has he removed our transgressions from us" (NIV). What a comfort to know that God has chosen to forget our sins! Could He remember if He chose to do so? God can do anything, anything except violate the restrictions He has placed on himself. For us humans, I don't believe our efforts should be placed on "trying to forget" the wrongs done. If we concentrate on forgiving, and being forgiven, then forgetting becomes more plausible—and less important. Eventually God takes the "sting" of hurts away as we faithfully seek His power to forgive wrongs done.

Pray As Christ Prayed

Forgiving a person who has wounded you, or even severely damaged you, can be most difficult. Unless you've experienced the stubborn nature of bitterness, it's hard to comprehend the process of wanting God's will, knowing that scripturally we have no choice but to forgive (Matthew 18:32–35, NIV), and yet feeling as if your prayers are bouncing off the ceiling.

It seems that Hebrews 12:15 was written specifically to help those who struggle with the consequences of bitterness: "See to it that no one comes *short of the grace of God; that no root of bitterness springing up causes trouble, and by it many be defiled* (emphasis added).

I have experienced firsthand the defiling work of harbored bitterness. Having been wronged by a person who never admitted the wrong—nor did that person request my forgiveness—I have lived with the consequence of unrelenting hatred toward a fellow human being. I found bitterness to be like a sticky super-glue that kept me bound to one spot in my life. Everything and everyone was tainted by my bitterness.

Neil T. Anderson says in his book *The Bondage Breakers*, "If you don't let offenders off your hook, you are hooked to them and the past, and that just means continued pain for you. Stop the pain; let it go. You don't forgive someone merely for their sake; you do it for *your* sake so you can be free. Your need to forgive isn't an issue between you and the offender; it's between you and God."[1]

Even though I was dealing with the aftermath of bitterness, I was also a Christian who was trying desperately hard to live up to the image of being a Bible-believing, evangelical Christian. I loved the Lord, but I came to realize that loving the Lord and hating a fellow human being were not compatible. (See 1 John 3:15; 4:7–8.) The Scriptures could not be any clearer than 1 John 4:20–21, which says, "If someone says, 'I love God,' and hates his brother, he is a liar; for the one who does not love his brother, whom he has seen, cannot love God, whom he has not seen. And this commandment we have from Him, that the one who loves God should love his brother also."

Bitterness and unforgiveness are not always demonstrated

[1]Neil T. Anderson, *The Bondage Breakers* (Eugene, Ore.: Harvest House Publishers, 1990), p. 196.

in such black-and-white terms. There are those of us who are bound by unforgiveness, but the manifestations of the anger are somewhat more subtle. Listen to Kim's story:

> I was molested throughout my childhood by my father. Even though I'm in my forties, I'm just now dealing with everything. I thought I had worked out all the emotional baggage during his illness and subsequent death a few years ago, but now I see that my life is dominated by the consequences of the molestation.
>
> All through my life, I've tried to control everything. I didn't tell anybody what was going on with my dad because I didn't want to upset anyone, especially my mother. I felt it was my responsibility to keep it all together and protect my mother. I'm in counseling now, and my counselor tells me I need to tell my mother what Dad did. I don't think I can do that. I've spent a lifetime protecting everyone, making sure everyone else is all right. Where has taking care of everyone else gotten me? I've completely worn myself out.
>
> After I got married, I never wanted to have children. I was afraid I'd abuse my children in the same way I was abused. Well, abuse comes in different ways, and what I feared is happening. I'm really abusing my children with worry right now. I find it impossible to trust God. I love Him, and I'm thankful that He has saved me, but I can't trust Him on a daily basis.
>
> One of my children has become so fearful that he doesn't want to spend the night away from home. Whenever I hear a siren, I'm convinced someone in my family has been in an accident. I'm always on edge, and it shows. My son asks me, "Why don't you trust God?" How do I tell him, "I can't trust God because He betrayed me and let something really bad happen to me"? I know being this honest may sound really terrible, but I'm trying to get help. Sweeping the problem under the rug and pretending has not helped in the past. I've decided to be honest for a change and really say how I feel.
>
> I've been through spiritual deliverance; I've prayed and been in counseling. It's not that I don't want to be free of all this junk; I just can't seem to get past it. But I'm not going to give up. There's too much at stake, not only for me but for my children. At this point, I'm not the only one who is suffering; my entire family is paying for the sins of my father.

Jana was abused by her stepfather during her growing-up years. Not so protective of her mother, she decided to tell her exactly what had happened. She was devastated to learn that her mother was not outraged, nor horrified. To her mother, this was "just something that happens" in some families. Jana's mother had been molested for many years by her father, and her mother before her by her father. The cycle of abuse had been perpetuated through several generations.

As Jana searched for answers, she found great solace and healing in the well-known words of King David as he pled for forgiveness: "Surely I was sinful at birth, sinful from the time my mother conceived me" (Psalm 51:5, NIV). Jana came to understand that she too was a sinner and needed forgiveness just as much as she needed to forgive the one who had abused her.

Jana's honest, up-front approach has helped her accept her past, forgive her stepfather, and work on the issues that pop up from time to time as a result of the abuse. For instance, Jana has a hard time letting her children out of her sight. Leaving her small son with a babysitter can be a real test of her trust in God. This has caused some conflict with her husband, who would like occasionally to have a night out as a couple rather than always going as a family. Meanwhile, her husband is trying to remain supportively understanding as Jana works on the trust factor.

Jana is determined that the abuse will stop with her generation. Jana's mother, however, has not dealt well with the aftermath of her own abuse. Instead of holding her father responsible, Jana blames her mother. Instead of talking honestly with her mother and sharing her feelings of anger, she is simply waiting for her to die. Jana says, "She believes all the pain will go away after her mother is gone." Sadly enough, the pain never does "just go away"; it has to be "put away."

Patricia Sprinkle, author of *Women Who Do Too Much*, said it well: "Another reason we don't forgive is that we feel justified in holding on to our grievances. What we don't realize is that the anger of unforgiveness is like acid destroying its container. We don't notice how blame and guilt slow down everything else we do by wearing out our bodies and consuming our days."[2]

---

[2]Patricia Sprinkle, *Women Who Do Too Much* (Grand Rapids, Mich.: Zondervan, 1992), p. 36.

This need to forgive is demonstrated in a song Steve and I wrote that will serve as a warning to those who fall into the trap of withholding forgiveness.

The Key[3]

I cannot tell you how I was hurt,
But I'll tell you I've had some tears;
I cannot tell you who it was that turned my trust into fears,
But I took the pieces of my broken heart,
And I built some prison walls,
And there I have held that offender for years,
And this is what I thought,
"He will never know freedom;
As long as I live I'll never give him freedom."

But then one day the Visitor came to this prison in my heart;
He said, "You ought to know the truth about the one behind
    the bars;
Yes, he's weak and he's weary and he has not smiled in years,
And you have been successful at keeping his eyes filled with
    tears."

"But, oh, how he longs for freedom!
These words are the key; they first came from Me;
Father, forgive them;
Come let me show you how to use them."

"Don't you know the offender is rarely the one in pain?
Instead, the one who will not forgive is the one who wears
    the chains."
So I opened up the prison door—
    I used forgiveness as the key,
And when I let the prisoner go, I found that it was me.

Oh, how sweet is the freedom!
It came on the day when my heart prayed,
"Father, forgive them; Father forgive them."

No one ever said that forgiving is easy. "Forgiveness is costly; we pay the price of the evil we forgive. Yet you're going to live with those consequences whether you want to or not; your only choice is whether you will do so in the bitterness of unforgive-

---

[3]Words and music by Steve and Annie Chapman, as recorded on *Reachable* CD (Times and Seasons Music, Inc. BMI, 1992). Used by permission.

ness or the freedom of forgiveness."[4] It is true that *forgiveness cost Christ His life, and forgiveness costs us our right to revenge.* As humans, we were not designed for the job of *judge.* When we take on the responsibilities of judge and jury, we are usurping the work of God. Hebrews 10:30–31 reminds us that God says, "Vengeance is Mine, I will repay." And again, "The Lord will judge His people. It is a terrifying thing to fall into the hands of the living God." Also, Romans 12:19 states, "Do not take revenge, my friends, but leave room for God's wrath, for it is written: 'It is mine to avenge; I will repay,' says the Lord" (NIV).

Popular culture asserts that revenge is good. An article in a recent issue of *Redbook* magazine stated, "An act of revenge is growth-promoting when it strengthens our sense of self, when it makes us feel that we deserve respect and can protect ourselves. . . . Revenge can be profoundly right, appropriate and deeply gratifying."[5] This idea of "healthy revenge" is profoundly wrong! We must resist these kinds of destructive outside forces, and turn to the only One who has the power to avenge.

Forgiving doesn't come naturally to us.

When Christ was on the cross dying for our sins, He showed us how to forgive. Christ was sinless and undeserving of the cross; however, in order for us to know forgiveness He willingly laid down His life for us. Looking down at those who were killing Him, He prayed, "Father, forgive them, for they do not know what they are doing" (Luke 23:34). By His prayer we learn that forgiveness is a divine act that requires a divine source. The source of that divine forgiveness is found in the Father. As Christ prayed "Father," calling on the source outside His own humanness, so we are to call beyond our own resources to forgive those who have hurt us. Anything we are called upon to forgive is small in comparison to what Christ forgave. "He made Him who knew no sin to be sin on our behalf, that we might become the righteousness of God in Him" (2 Corinthians 5:21). What a burden for one so pure to pay the price for Kim's molesting father, and Jana's despicable stepfather, and your sin, and my sin. He showed us, by the example of His prayer from the cross, *how* to forgive, and through the acceptable sacrifice of His very life, He

---

[4]Anderson, op. cit.
[5]Judith Viorst, "Revenge—How Sweet It Is," *Redbook* (July 1991).

has provided the *power* to forgive.

Christ is our only hope to be reconciled to God. Hebrews 9:22–28 tells us the good news. He has forgiven our past sin; when He died on the cross, He sacrificed himself once and for all (9:26); He has given us the Holy Spirit to help us deal with present sin; He appears for us now in heaven as our high priest (9:24); and He promises to return (9:28) and raise us to eternal life in the world where sin will be banished. (Life Application Bible, Tyndale Press.)

You may be caught in the tangled web of unforgiveness and bitterness. How do you forgive someone who has hurt you badly? The damage may be incomprehensible, but let me point you to the One who suffered beyond our ability to understand. His suffering was to provide our forgiveness and salvation. Only until we understand how very much we have been forgiven will we be able to extend forgiveness to another. (See Luke 7:47.)

Steps to Forgiveness

Be honest.

As an act of your will, allow Jesus to walk into that room in your heart where lie your broken dreams, hurt feelings, and betrayed trust. Open the door and let Him take an honest look at what has happened to you. "Acknowledge the hurt and hate. If your forgiveness doesn't visit the emotional core of your past, it will be incomplete. This is the great evangelical cover-up. Christians feel the pain of interpersonal offenses, but we won't acknowledge it. Let God bring the pain to the surface so He can deal with it. This is where the healing takes place."[6]

The Secret Place[7]

My heart is like a house; one day I let the Savior in,
And there are many rooms,
Where He would visit now and then;
But then one day He saw that door;
I knew the day had come too soon.
I said, "Jesus, I'm not ready, for us to visit in that room.

---

[6]Anderson, op. cit.
[7]Words and music by Steve Chapman, as recorded on *Reachable* CD (Dawn Treader Music, a division of Jubilee Communications, Inc., SESAC, 1980). Used by permission.

'Cause that's a place in my heart where even I don't go;
I have some things hidden there,
I don't want anyone to know."
But He handed me the keys, with tears of love on His face;
He said, "I want to make you clean;
Let me go in your secret place."

So I opened up the door, and as the two of us walked in
I was so ashamed; His light revealed my hidden sin;
But when I think about that room now,
I'm not afraid anymore
'Cause I know my hidden sin,
   no longer hides behind that door.

That was a place in my heart where even I didn't go;
I had some things hidden there;
I didn't want anyone to know;
But He handed me the keys, with tears of love on His face;
He made me clean, I let Him in my secret place.

Is there a place in your heart where even you don't go?

Be prayerful.

Ephesians 6:11–13 and 18 tells us *how* we should fight in order to win: "Put on the full armor of God, that you may be able to stand firm against the schemes of the devil. For our struggle is not against flesh and blood, but against the rulers, against the powers, against the world-forces of this darkness, against the spiritual forces of wickedness in the heavenly places. Therefore, take up the full armor of God, that you may be able to resist in the evil day, and having done everything, to stand firm. . . . With all prayer and petition pray at all times in the Spirit, and with this in view, be on the alert with all perseverance and petition for all the saints." Note that the "flesh and blood" reference in verse 12 means that those who are NOT "flesh and blood" are demons over whom Satan has control. We need a supernatural power to defeat Satan, and God has provided this by giving us His Holy Spirit within us and His armor surrounding us.

The attacks of the enemy may come through people who are supposed to love and protect us. When Joseph's brothers plotted his murder, only to change their minds and sell him into slavery, his life was permanently altered. By the evil actions of his brothers, he was rendered a captive to the enemy, falsely accused, and put into prison. He lost the love of his father, the companionship of his brother Benjamin, his language, his religion, and his inheritance, as well as his physical freedom.

Even though terrible things happened to him by the hands of his brothers, Joseph knew the One who ultimately controlled his future. In Genesis 50:20 Joseph tells his brothers, "And as for you, you meant evil against me, but God meant it for good in order to bring about this present result. . . ."

You may have suffered at the hands of those who were supposed to love you. Because of the evilness of their deeds, you have been rendered a captive to the enemy of your soul. You have lost more than anyone could know. You may even be suffering physical repercussions because of the harm done. Through prayer, keep dedicating yourself to the One who judges righteously (1 Peter 2:23). Ask God to show you, even as He showed Joseph, what good He wants to bring out of the evil others intended.

Just as in the case of Joseph, our pain is not wasted. Second Corinthians 1:3–5 encourages us, "Blessed be the God and Father of our Lord Jesus Christ, the Father of mercies and God of all comfort; who comforts us *in all our affliction* so that we may be able to comfort those who are in any affliction with the comfort with which we ourselves are comforted by God. For just as the *sufferings* of Christ are ours in abundance, so also our comfort is abundant through Christ" (emphasis added).

While some suffer because of the actions of others, some of us deal with anger and bitterness toward God because of foolish decisions *we* have made. Ultimately, that leaves us with a lifetime of regret. A young couple who were not yet married prayed on the way to a motel, "Lord, if you don't want us to have sex, then make our car have a flat tire." When no such event occurred and the young woman got pregnant, they were disappointed with God, because, after all, they had prayed. Was God at fault? God had already given them the instruction that they needed. First Corinthians 6:13 says, "But sexual sin is never right: our bodies were not made for that, but for the Lord, and the Lord wants to fill our bodies with himself" (TLB).

Instead of blaming God for our problems, some of us need to be honest with Him and with ourselves. Prayerfully ask God to bring good from your situation, then walk in forgiveness.

Forgive and keep on forgiving.

You may have to pray a hundred times a day for that one who hurt you, but go ahead and pray. Matthew 18:21–22 says, " 'Lord, how often shall my brother sin against me and I forgive him? Up to seven times?' Jesus said to him, 'I don't say to you, up to seven times, but up to seventy times seven.' " Christ has provided the means and the power to forgive. He has shown us our responsibility to forgive, and the benefit of forgiving. The only thing left for us to do is persevere.

Hebrews 10:36 encourages us: "You need to persevere so that when you have done the will of God, you will receive what he has promised" (NIV).

Don't think that forgiveness is simply a one-time act. Forgiveness is something you have to do every time you think of another infraction, or when the old feelings start to resurface.

If your husband had an affair, you may well have to forgive him every time you think of that "other woman." One friend of mine forgave her husband for an adulterous affair. She said when she took him back she didn't realize just how many times she would have to forgive him. When the bills started coming in for an exotic vacation trip he had taken with his "girlfriend," she had to forgive him every time a dime of their money went for that charge card bill. God forgives us and we must forgive others.

Getting back to Ken and Kathy: After Ken had asked for forgiveness, I then turned to Kathy and said, "Now, you ask him to forgive you." (Being told to ask for forgiveness is very scriptural, since 1 John 1:9 instructs us to do that very thing.) Being a close friend of Kathy, I knew their marital problems were not just a one-way street. They had both done their share of hurting. The tears started to come as she asked for his forgiveness. With eyes of love he readily forgave her.

They both promised there would be no more "beating each other up with past sins"—no bringing up the past no matter how angry either of them got.

The commitment to put the past behind them and deal with the present seemed a relief to them both. We sent them home with a prayer and a promise to continue to pray. Embracing a spirit of humility, of continual forgiveness, and of resistance to the spiritual forces that would seek to destroy them is the only hope for this family.

There is great hope for Ken and Kathy, and there is great hope for you and your family as well. Christ has paved the way; now we must walk in it. The path is not easy, but it will lead to freedom.

8

Too Young to Die Old

A little boy walked up and enthusiastically announced that it was his birthday. The joy of aging was almost more than he could bear. "And how old are you today?" I inquired, my eyes wide with excitement to mirror his.

"I'm this many," he said as he held up four chubby fingers.

"Wow! I can't believe you're four years old. Are you married yet?"

He replied with an air of sincerity, "No, not yet."

The sweet conversation with that young man served to remind me that aging is indeed an attitude, rather than just an accumulation of chronological years. To the little boy, being four years old was something to "crow" about. (In my case the word "crow" also comes up, but it's more in line with "crow's feet.")

When my son, Nathan, turned thirteen he was ecstatic to finally be a teenager and too old to order off the children's menu. (For some reason he had found that totally humiliating.) When Steve turned forty, I celebrated his birthday with an "over-the-hill" party. I decorated the house with the proverbial black balloons, the guests wore black, and he received gifts such as anti-wrinkle cream, Absorbine Jr., and Preparation-H. I had a great time at his expense, forgetting, of course, that ten months later he would have the chance to get me back!

Turning forty was a sobering experience. It seemed so old at the time, but now the farther I get from it, the younger it sounds. You know the old saying: "Age is a matter of the mind. If you don't mind, it doesn't matter."

There's another old saying that from ages one to twenty-one, we do what somebody else tells us to do; from ages twenty-one to sixty-five, we do what we have to do; but from sixty-five on, we get to do what we want to do. If this is true, then I'm definitely at the age when I find myself on "automatic pilot"—doing what I *have* to do. But I'm looking forward to sixty-five and beyond when I get to do what I *want*.

To be perfectly honest, though, I'm *not* looking forward to watching my face slide off my chin and my chest flap against my belly button. Even though I'm only in my mid-forties, I can already see and feel the aging process at work. Sir Isaac Newton was right on when he discovered the cold, hard reality of gravity: That which was once up does definitely come down.

How do we deal with the reality of aging in a society that puts such a high premium on youthful good looks? Women are especially affected by this unfair attitude toward aging. There is little question who is more valued in our society: a woman with laugh lines and the ability to carry on an intelligent conversation, or a woman with a firm behind. Most men over the age of fifty, with a touch of gray at the temple, accentuated with a few wrinkles and crinkles, are valued for their experience, wisdom, and position. Women who show their age, on the other hand, have to fight the stereotype of being considered "three days older than dirt." It is without question unfair that aging men are considered "distinguished," while aging women are considered "extinguished."

Lloyd Ogilvie gives a refreshing perspective on aging in his book *If God Cares, Why Do I Still Have Problems?*

> So many of us are old before our time. In fact, I have come to believe that "oldness" is not a matter of age at all. It's a condition of the mind. I know some young adults who have geriatric attitudes while still in their middle twenties. And I know people in their forties who have stopped enjoying life and are not growing intellectually or spiritually. Some of my friends who are in their fifties act grim and gray. On the other hand, I know some chronologically older people who have a youthful vibrancy about them. They may be in the winter season by age, but they have never lost the

spring of enthusiasm in their hearts.[1]

In the November 1994 issue of the *Ladies' Home Journal*, a survey of over fifteen hundred women in the Baby Boomer generation (thirties and forties) were asked, "What's the best thing about getting older?" Thirty-four percent said the best thing about the passing years was they knew more than they used to. Thirty-three percent said their lives were more settled, and twenty-three percent felt better about themselves.

In the same survey, the question was asked, "What's the worst thing about getting older?" Extra pounds headed the list of concerns: Forty-two percent said gaining weight was at the top. Eighteen percent complained of wrinkles as being the worst part of aging.

Being Old; Thinking Young

Lillian has accomplished a lot in her lifetime. Through abundance of effort, she and her husband of forty-eight years, Paul, have raised two wonderful children. They continue to enjoy their five extraordinary grandchildren, and boast of two beautiful great-grandchildren.

Lillian's heart of service has reached well beyond the walls of her own home. She and Paul pastored for over thirty years and have done evangelistic work in numerous other churches. Without question the main attraction I have for Lillian is in regard to the excellent job she did in raising my husband. As I have said before, my mother-in-law is a great example of a positive person. Her positive outlook on life carries over into the area of aging. Listen to what she has to say about facing her senior years:

> I am a senior citizen. I don't mind admitting it, either. When I stand in front of the mirror I see wrinkles and all the ways my body has changed through the years, and there's only one thing I can say: "Lillian, you are fearfully and wonderfully made."
>
> I treat my body really well. I've been *walking* every day, come rain or come shine, for three years. I try to *eat the right*

---

[1]Lloyd Ogilvie, *If God Cares, Why Do I Still Have Problems?* (Waco, Tex.: Word Books, 1985), p. 123.

foods. I'm a little heavier than I want to be right now, but the extra weight will come off. I try to *put good things in my mind.* I *feed my mind on the Word of God* every day, and keep a positive attitude. I try to *talk about good things with people.* If I get mad at somebody, I go in and kneel down beside my bed and I pray, "Lord, this person made me so mad, I can't stand it. And now, I'm going to loose them and give them to you." I then get up and feel better in my mind and body. *I leave my anger there with the Lord.* I have to do that quite often. Taking every thought captive to the obedience of Christ is the key to treating your body and mind well. When you get older you learn to appreciate having a sound body and a sound mind and you do whatever it takes to keep them sound. This reminds me of something I heard said: "If I'd known I was going to live so long, I would have taken better care of myself." *I don't want to wait and pay later.*

P.J. and I pastored for twenty-five years and then retired from that church. I thought, "Lord, is this all you have for me? I don't want to quit; I want my life to be more fruitful in my older years than in my younger." God has answered that prayer and has opened doors for me to minister to others. I feel like I really make a difference. I volunteer at the nursing home in the town in which I live. I've learned a lot from the old people there, but most of all *I've learned how not to act.*

Older people are just like teenagers. We all are trying to cope with our age. Teenagers have peer pressure, but so do we "keenagers." (Isn't that what they should call those of us who are packed full of wisdom?) We worry about being loved and accepted. We worry about fitting in with our group of friends. In a way, things really don't change a whole lot through the years. Perhaps the one advantage we older people have over the younger is our broader view of life. Our perspective is bigger because we've learned the truth that *good times don't last forever, but neither do bad times.*

My advice to women who are dealing with the passage of time would be the same advice I gave my husband one day after I had spent some time with the "old folks" in the nursing home. I said, "P.J., let's think young." The next Sunday, my husband got up in church and told the congregation what I had said. His response was not exactly what I had in mind. He told the church, "My wife wants us to start thinking young, so I think I'm gonna get me a Boy Scout uniform and start helping little old ladies across the street."

Before we explore how to think young, let's first look at what thinking old is like. You may be old at forty and young at eighty, but you are genuinely old at any age if:

- You feel old.
- You feel you have learned all there is to learn.
- You find yourself saying, "I'm too old to do that."
- You feel tomorrow has no promise.
- You take no interest in the activities of youth.
- You would rather talk than listen.
- You long for the "good old days," feeling they were the best.[2]

If any one of these statements describes your state of mind, regardless of your age, please stop right now. Starting this day, learn to think young! If Lillian is an example of thinking young, you will be pleased with the results.

As far as I'm concerned, I'm not old. I heard one time that "old" is fifteen years older than you are. If that's the case, then we should never really feel old. Douglas MacArthur said it well:

Nobody grows old by merely living a number of years. People grow old by deserting their ideals. Years may wrinkle the skin, but to give up interest wrinkles the soul. Worry, doubt, self-distrust, fear and despair . . . these are the long, long years that bow the head and turn the growing spirit back to dust.

Whatever your years, there is in every being's heart the love of wonder, the undaunted challenge of events, the unfailing, childlike appetite for "what next," and the joy of the game of life.

You are as young as your faith, as old as your doubt; as young as your self-confidence, as old as your fear; as young as your hope, as old as your despair.

A recent *Nightline* news program made reference to research that encourages the elderly to keep feeding their minds new information (new hobbies, activities, reading materials, conversation), for in doing so, the chances of developing Alzheimer's disease decreases. Therefore, part of thinking young means continuously feeding our minds with new information.

---

[2]Taken from *Encyclopedia of 7700 Illustrations* (Rockville, Md.: Assurance Publishers, 1979).

Thinking young means you see life as:

POSSIBILITIES NOT PROBLEMS
OPPORTUNITIES NOT OBSTACLES
HUMOR NOT HORROR

Possibilities Not Problems

Thinking young means wanting to effect change. Women who have completed the job of mothering, as well as women whose spouses have gone on to be with the Lord, need not sit in a rocking chair and wait to die. Titus 2:3–4 warns against the temptation of misusing our time in our later years: "Older women likewise are to be reverent in their behavior, not malicious gossips, nor enslaved to much wine, teaching what is good, that they may encourage the young women. . . ."

Thinking young is essential for those who are growing older. Remember, growing older is still growing. When people reach sixty-five they are not automatically freeze-dried with all opportunities for learning, giving, and receiving taken away. Learning and improving must continue throughout all ages. Maintaining an anticipation about the future is an important part of thinking young.

Philadelphia was the home of sixty-seven-year-old Margaret Kuhn when she organized a group of five friends, all retired church workers from different denominations, known as the Gray Panthers. This group, together with a team of lawyers, investigated nursing homes and lobbied in Congress for better legislation to protect the aged. Miss Kuhn said, "Much of senility is not irreversible; it is induced by despair and frustration. Fixed retirement is dehumanizing. It shows how stupid our society is in making scrap piles of the elderly. We're not mellow, sweet old people. We've got time to effect change and nothing to lose."

Maintaining the ability to keep looking at possibilities instead of problems can be challenging, especially when faced with the devastating trauma of losing a spouse. Maggie seemed totally unprepared and unable to cope with life after the death of her beloved husband, James.

Even though her children and grandchildren tried to cheer her up, it was obvious that her "treasure" was in heaven, and this old world was nothing but a burden to her.

When a simple cold turned into pneumonia a few months after her husband's death, she seemed to lack the will to fight it. We were all saddened when she died unexpectedly, following James in death just seven months later.

How sad to see someone lose their vision for the future because they continue to only look back. Keeping an eye on the future can make all the difference.

After a concert, Steve and I met a beautiful couple in their mid-sixties. Their striking good looks seemed to complement each other. Thinking them to be married a number of years, we were surprised to learn they were just dating. They shared their story, and Steve wrote it down in lyric form. This couple discovered a renewed purpose in life, together.

They Never Dreamed[3]

He passed away some time ago,
Washed her dreams away in tears;
She thought she'd be a widow for the rest of her years,
But then one day her sister called,
"Could you come here Tuesday night?"
There'll be four of us in all;
We think he's someone you might like.

She'd been through that scheme before,
Another evening on display,
She'd go along, just one more time,
It wasn't easy at her age;
But right away, she realized,
He was not like all the rest;
He put a smile back in her eyes;
She wondered if she passed the test.

She never dreamed she'd dream that way again
'Cause when the evening was over,
All she thought about was him
And how they came so quickly to feel like lifetime friends;
She never dreamed she'd dream that way again.

She didn't know the thoughts he had
When he went back to his room;
It'd been a while since he felt like that,

---

[3]Words and music by Steve Chapman, as recorded on *Waiting to Hear* CD (Times and Seasons Music, Inc., BMI, 1994). Used by permission.

And he wondered if she knew
That he shared the pain that she had known
When Heaven called his love away;
He placed her number by the phone
And rehearsed what he would say.

And he never dreamed he'd dream that way again;
When the evening was over all he thought about was them
And how they came so quickly to feel like lifetime friends;
He never dreamed he'd dream that way again.

She never dreamed she'd dream that way again;
He never dreamed he'd dream that way again;
They never dreamed they'd dream that way again.

Opportunities Not Obstacles

When God called Moses to lead the Israelites out of Egypt at age eighty, Moses made lots of excuses, but being too old was not one of them. If a person is in reasonably good health, age should not be a deterrent to serving God.

John Wesley traveled two hundred fifty miles a day for forty years. He preached forty thousand sermons, produced four hundred books, and spoke ten languages. At age eighty-three, he was annoyed that he could not write more than fifteen hours a day without hurting his eyes. Upon reaching his eighty-sixth year, he was ashamed he could not preach more than twice a day.

On his eighty-fifth birthday, John Wesley wrote in his diary:

I find some decay in my memory with regard to names and things lately past, but not at all with what I read twenty, forty, sixty, years ago. Nor do I feel any weariness, either in traveling or preaching. To what cause can I impute this? First, to the power of God, fitting me to the work to which I am called; and next, to the prayers of His children. Then, may not I impute it to these inferior means:

1. My constant exercise and change of air.

2. My never having lost a night's sleep, sick or well, on land or at sea.

3. My having slept at will, whether day or night.

4. My having risen constantly at 4:00 A.M. for about sixty years.

5. My constant preaching at 5:00 A.M. for about fifty years.

6. My having so little pain, sorrow, or anxious care in life.

Corrie ten Boom did not allow herself to be limited by age. Even though she had suffered severely in a Nazi concentration camp (for helping Jews escape certain death), this sweet little lady's influence was felt around the world. Taking the message of unconditional forgiveness and redemption to a hurting world at age eighty-five, she continued her traveling ministry even after having a pacemaker implanted into her failing heart. She ministered until April 15, 1983, when she peacefully passed into the presence of the Lord she loved on her ninety-first birthday.

Mother Teresa is a modern-day example of a woman in her eighties who shames us all with her relentless fight for the outcasts of Calcutta, India. Raised in an affluent home, she gave up a comfortable life to wipe the fevered brows of the dying and feed the starving people of a foreign country. Age has not hindered her from making an enormous difference in her world.

Many of history's most celebrated individuals were well up in years, and still going strong, while accomplishing great things. Michelangelo was still composing poetry and designing structures in his eighty-ninth year. Richard Strauss was still composing serious music after his eightieth birthday. Benjamin Franklin began writing his autobiography at age sixty-five, went to France in the service of his country at age seventy, and helped to draft the Constitution of the United States at age eighty-one.

John Milton, although blind, completed *Paradise Lost* when he was fifty-nine, and *Paradise Regained* at sixty-three. Alfred Lord Tennyson wrote "Crossing the Bar" at age eighty-three.

Grandma Moses, the great American artist, began painting at age seventy-six and sold her first painting at age seventy-eight. She had her first art show at age eighty. At ninety-five, she was commissioned to do a painting for the White House, and at the ripe "young" age of one hundred, she illustrated the now-classic "Visit from Saint Nicholas."

Age need not ever be an excuse for nonproductive living. Our latter years, without the demands of raising a family and carrying on the responsibilities of full-time employment, should be greater years than our former.

Humor Not Horror

Of course, aging can be a frightening thing to face. Seeing your face and body change, feeling your movements becoming more restricted, and knowing your mind is slipping are no laughing matters. However, keeping a sense of humor can be the best gift you give yourself as you get older. Proverb 17:22 says, "A joyful heart is good medicine, but a broken spirit dries up the bones." A good old-fashioned belly laugh may be what you need to get through another day. I love the old poem that says:

I am fully aware that my youth has been spent.
That my get up and go has got up and went.
But I really don't mind, when I think with a grin,
Of all the good places my get up has been.

Facing the inevitable process of aging with a sense of humor can make it not only a tolerable experience, but one that can bring us great joy and a sense of renewed purpose.

Erma Bombeck tells about seeing an old friend, with whom she had shared many of the same heartaches and disappointments. Read how she expresses even the tragedies of failing health and aging.

We fought gravity together, dyed our hair together. . . . Throughout our lives, we could always depend on each other to be supportive and say the right thing. When she got breast cancer, I wept. When I got breast cancer, she cried. Our letters and phone calls had gone beyond, "How are the kids?"

. . . The physical and emotional scars covered both our bodies. The stretch marks, the Caesarean tracks, the loss of a child and death of parents, the moon-face from taking prednisone, the water retention of kidney failure, the prostheses, the gray roots that grew at the rate of two inches a week. Was it possible we had weathered it all and remained intact? Yes!

"You haven't changed a bit," I shouted as we embraced. "My goodness, you are still the same," she said with relief. . . . Once more we proved what we all know—friendship is blind.[4]

---

[4]Erma Bombeck, "Light Housekeeping," *Good Housekeeping* (February 1994).

I am confident that God answers the prayer of Psalm 71 for those who are facing the senior years. "Do not cast me away when I am old; do not forsake me when my strength is gone. . . . Even when I am old and gray, do not forsake me, O God. . . ." (vv. 9, 18, NIV).

Older but Better

Like it or not, America is getting older. In his book *Wise and Wonderful*, Charles L. Allen says: "In 1900, a newborn could expect to live to age forty-seven; a newborn today can be expected to live to age seventy-five. Better living conditions, increased understanding of our human problems, medical science and other factors are lengthening human life."[5]

These days, however, getting older doesn't necessarily mean being sick or unhealthy. People are taking better care of themselves. Many older people are eating healthier foods and getting helpful exercise. With our increased health consciousness, we're seeing legislation to create a healthier environment—such as smoke-free public buildings—and greater access to preventive health care. With such measures, perhaps future older generations will not only grow older and wiser, but will also look and feel better in the process.

Older Doesn't Have to Mean Dependent

I was surprised to learn in Charles Allen's book that four out of five elderly people live independently. About one-third of elderly people do, however, live alone. And even in the group of people over the age of eighty-five, about half maintain independent households.[6]

At age eighty-six, my aunt Inez still lives independently in her own home. She makes beautiful quilts and crafts galore, cans fruits and vegetables from her garden, and bakes the best apple dumplings known to mankind. She is a glowing example of a woman who is elderly but doesn't act her age.

For many older people, maintaining independence is an es-

---

[5]Charles L. Allen, *Wise and Wonderful* (Grand Rapids, Mich.: Fleming H. Revell, 1994), p. 10.
[6]Ibid., p. 4.

sential part of being content and happy. We should not only be concerned with the years of our life, but also the life of our years. Leviticus 19:32 says, "Thou shalt rise up before the [gray] head, and honor the face of the old man [or old woman]" (KJV). In other words, *worth does not diminish as years increase.*

Trading Places

Dealing with aging in ourselves and our loved ones can be very difficult. Those adult children who have faced the painful experience of witnessing "the child becoming the parent, and the parent becoming the child" may relate to this song:[7]

"It's cold outside, put on your sweater,
Take your medicine, it will help you feel better."
These were Mama's words so long ago;
I hear them again, I hear them echo.

Oh, but this time they come from me
Every time I go to see her;
Yesterday I helped her tie her laces,
Then I realized, we were mother and child
Trading places.

"Let's cross the street, take hold of my hand,
When we're in the store, stay as close as you can."
When Mama said these words, love was the reason,
And still it is love, whenever she hears them.

Oh, but this time they come from me
Every time I go to see her;
Yesterday I helped her tie her laces,
Then I realized, we were mother and child
Trading places.

If my time goes on, I know there'll come a day,
When it will be my turn to hear my children say,

"It's cold outside, put on your sweater,
Take your medicine, it'll help you feel better."
These were Mama's words, so long ago;
I hear them again, I hear them echo.

---

[7]Words and music of "Trading Places" by Steve Chapman, as recorded on *A Mother's Touch* CD (Times and Seasons Music, Inc., BMI, 1994). Used by permission.

God's provision and grace are ever present, regardless of age, or regardless of health conditions. It is a comfort to know that the words of the psalmist David ring throughout all time, finding a place in our hearts, and encouraging us to the very end.

> The steps of a man [or woman] are established by the Lord; And He delights in his way. When he falls, he shall not be hurled headlong; because the Lord is the One who holds his hand. I have been young, and now I am old; Yet I have not seen the righteous forsaken, or his descendants begging bread. All day long he is gracious and lends; and his descendants are a blessing. (Psalm 37:23–26)

Anonymous Prayer

Lord, Thou knowest better than I know myself that I am growing old and someday will be old.

Keep me from getting talkative, and particularly from the fatal habit of thinking I must say something on every subject and on every occasion.

Release me from craving to try to straighten out everyone's affairs.

Keep my mind free from the recital of endless details— give me wings to get to the point.

I ask for grace enough to listen to the tales of others' pain—they are increasing and my love of rehearsing them is becoming sweeter as the years go by.

Teach me the glorious lesson that occasionally it is possible that I may be mistaken.

Keep me reasonably sweet; I do not want to be a saint— some of them are hard to live with—but a sour old woman is one of the crowning works of the devil.

Make me thoughtful, but not moody; helpful, but not bossy.

With my vast store of wisdom, it seems a pity not to use it all—but Thou knowest, Lord, that I want a few friends at the end.

As I read this prayer over and over, I see it is not only appropriate for the very old but for all of us. May God protect us— at any age—from using our limitations as an excuse for sloppy living.

"Even to your old age, I shall be the same, and even to your graying years I shall bear you!" (Isaiah 46:4a, NASB).

So let's not lose heart. The best is yet to come!

9

Yes, Lord, but I Never Counted on This!

Why do bad things happen? Why do babies die and spouses betray our love? Why do mothers get sick and daddies go away? These "detours" from what we expect out of life can suck the very heart out of us. When we are traveling down the road of life and the energy gauge is already registering on "E," where do we turn when a detour sign takes us down a path for which we are not prepared?

The story is told of an old farmer who was leisurely traveling down a country road. He was riding in a wagon pulled by an old mule. Sitting alongside him on the wagon seat was his favorite dog. A city slicker in a fancy sports car came up over a rise, going at a considerable speed. Not expecting to see such a sight, the city slicker plowed right over the old farmer, leaving quite a mess in the middle of the road. He then sped away, with the farmer pinned under the wagon.

Before long another car drove up. The farmer was relieved to see it was the state police. The state trooper walked over to one side of the road and discovered the old mule lying in the ditch. The mule was obviously in great pain, so to relieve the animal's suffering, the officer took out his revolver and shot the mule. He then walked over to the other side of the road and found the old dog lying in the other ditch, also suffering badly. So once again, the officer took his revolver and shot the dog.

The trooper continued to survey the situation and discovered the old farmer lying on the ground, under the wagon and unable to move. The trooper got down on his hands and knees and inquired of the farmer, "And sir, how are you feeling?"

Having just witnessed the previous acts of mercy by the trooper, the old farmer quickly declared, "I've never felt better in my life!"

Many of us are like that old farmer. On the outside we're saying, "I've never felt better in my life," but in our heart of hearts, we're pinned under a wagonload of hurt.

The degree and types of trouble may vary from one person to another, but one thing's for certain: In this world we will have tribulation (John 16:33). Whatever "load" has you immobilized, find comfort in this fact: *You are not alone.*

Real People; Real Problems

Charles and Mary appeared to have it all together. Married for over thirty years, with five children and four grandchildren, this couple taught Sunday school, helped with the missions program, and counseled struggling couples with their marital difficulties. Life had its ups and downs, but everything was going as usual, or so it seemed.

Mary told me her story:

> Charles hasn't really been a loving part of my life for the past ten years. I've never told anyone, not even my own mother, but there's been no real companionship for a long time. The more lonely I've felt, the more I've prayed. During one of my prayer times, I felt the Lord speak to my heart, "Every time Charles hurts you, I will kiss the hurt away."
>
> I have to admit that God has kept His promise. The loneliness and rejection have been soothed as God has revealed His love to me. The Lord has been faithful to me throughout the difficult times of my marriage.
>
> But the rug was really jerked out from under me when I discovered Charles had been having an affair with his secretary for the past couple of years. I never thought Charles would be unfaithful. He's been so harshly critical of people

we know who have committed adultery. His utter disdain of this sin led me to believe he'd never betray me in this way. (Perhaps his overly judgmental attitude was what opened the door to this happening in our marriage.)

Did I expect to be divorced after all these years, living in a small house after having had a large, beautiful home, plus being left with the total responsibility of raising our two youngest children by myself? No. Did I expect to be working two jobs, trying to make ends meet? No, I never counted on this!

In another home. . . .

Curtis had just returned home after serving in the Persian Gulf during Operation Desert Storm. Being reunited with his wife, Janice, and four-month-old son, Jeremy, was a dream come true.

Jeremy was a healthy, playful little boy who had taken Curtis' and Janice's hearts captive.

One morning the alarm went off, and Janice went into Jeremy's room to start the usual morning routine of changing his diaper, dressing, and feeding him. But when Janice looked at Jeremy, his little eyes were staring, his body blue and somewhat rigid.

Cuddling the baby in her arms, Janice took him to her bed. With a raspy voice, hardly able to utter the words, she said, "Curtis, wake up! We have to take Jeremy to the hospital."

In shock, Curtis looked at his son, stroked his soft little head, and cried in despair, "My God! He's dead!"

On the way to the hospital, Curtis was crying so hard he could hardly see to drive. But Janice never cried a tear.

In the emergency room Janice stood to one side holding the baby. When the nurses tried to take the baby from her arms, she only held him closer.

As the hours passed, their family doctor, grandparents, church family, and pastor came to their side. Janice, stone-faced, continued to rock Jeremy, refusing to relinquish her hold on the dead baby. Unaware of the pleading from family and friends, Janice continued to hold Jeremy well into the day. Eventually, the baby was taken from her arms.

It was weeks before Janice could think of packing up the nursery. Not only had her little boy died of SIDS (Sudden Infant Death Syndrome), but also gone were her hopes of having a family and the dreams for her first son.

Curtis and Janice found it difficult to talk about their son. Each grieved, but each grieved alone; their hurts were too deep to verbalize. Finally, one day Curtis asked Janice the question that opened the floodgates of emotion: "Janice, do you think it was your fault that Jeremy died?"

Bitter tears flowed. Yes, Janice blamed herself; she blamed God; she blamed Curtis; she blamed other couples whose babies were alive and healthy. The disappointment and loss were overwhelming. How could this happen? Dealing with the loss of her son was something Janice never counted on, and facing that loss stretched her to her limits.

Suffering Saint

Becky Romero is an attractive woman of Italian descent. She married her husband, Ed, after his first wife died giving birth to their seventh child. Having recently returned from the mission field, Becky stepped into the role of wife and mother with a real sense of purpose. Within time, Becky and Ed had two children of their own.

Becky was and is a woman of vision. She put feet, hands, and heart behind the relentless work of the pro-life agenda. Becoming a very effective lobbyist who gained the respect of both political parties, Becky also did not lack enemies. Those who oppose the protection of the unborn were vicious in their attacks on Mrs. Romero. Eventually, those attacks splashed over to her husband, Ed, who was a successful physician.

When a young woman died in the emergency room under Dr. Romero's care, the local newspaper assaulted him with a continuous barrage of articles. Becky knew her husband was being heartlessly pummeled because of her political and moral stands. When the unfair editorials appeared day after day, Becky would get down on her knees and beg Ed for forgiveness. Ed never blamed Becky nor backed away from his own convictions.

With mounting public pressure, spearheaded by the biased media, Ed lost the malpractice suit and his insurance was canceled. The Romeros now have no means of income other than being financially supported by family members. Becky's health has suffered to the place where she is unable to leave her home. They have been forced to sell their properties, and their oldest son has had to leave college for lack of funds.

Becky and her family have suffered financially and personally for doing what is right. Somewhere in the midst of our modern-day theology which insinuates that "if we do right, good things will happen to us" is the uncomfortable reality that there really are Christians who sacrifice all they have for their principles, only to find themselves thrown into the "lions' den" of suffering.

When Becky took on the fight for the unborn, she did not know that those she loved would be ruined financially and personally humiliated. She had and still has complete belief in God's goodness and love. But everything she has suffered has caused her to say, "Yes, Lord, but I never counted on this!"

In Sickness . . .

When Daniel and Karla married twenty years ago, they moved to Nashville. Karla found an excellent job and eagerly entered into her profession with the same sense of excitement and enthusiasm with which she approached every area of her life. A high achiever, energetic and capable, she tackled her responsibilities as administrative assistant with great gusto.

Even though she was experiencing tremendous success and encouragement in her job, she kept feeling that the Lord wanted to do more with her life. She sensed that God wanted her to slow down and have children, but she resisted.

Karla said:

> I kept on saying no to the Lord's nudging to slow down. I loved my job and thought I could handle it. I definitely did not want to quit working. My attitude changed when my father had a heart attack. It was only when I faced the possibility of losing my dad that I realized I wanted my father to know my children. (The Lord was gracious to give me a second chance, and eleven more years with my father.)
>
> Before long, I got pregnant, and within a few years we had three daughters. For a while I was able to keep up with my career and growing family. Somehow, I had gotten onto the "rat-race track" and I didn't know how to get off. I was doing it all, and it was doing me in. I've now learned that if we don't know how to stop, sometimes God will stop us.

That's what He did with me, and unfortunately, I learned it the hard way.

About four and half years ago I contracted a virus that would not go away. It was like the flu, twenty-four hours a day, every single day. The doctors couldn't find out what was wrong with me, even though they ran test after test. I ended up unable to get out of bed. Trying to raise children and run a household is not easy when you're confined to a bed. But I couldn't have gotten up if I'd wanted to; I literally could not move.

Even though my whole body ached constantly and I had no energy, the doctors still couldn't diagnose my illness. It took nine months before I could gather the strength to go to the grocery store. If I did manage to go to the store, that would be all I was able to do that day. A couple of times I managed to get into the car, but forgot where I was and where I wanted to go.

I can't adequately express the frustration of being rendered unable to do anything, after being a driven, high-energy, high-intensity person. My body had turned on me—it had simply shut down, and I was powerless to force it to function. I was finally diagnosed as having Chronic Fatigue Immune Deficiency Syndrome. Having a name for my illness helped somewhat, but it didn't help me regain my energy level, or my memory, which I had lost for the most part. Being an avid reader, it was painful to realize I couldn't comprehend what I was reading nor retain what I had read in the past. My identity was being taken from me; the person I considered myself to be was no longer there.

For the first time in my life, God had my full attention. I was no longer able to run from Him. I didn't have the energy or strength to do anything on my own. There was only one thing I could do. Each day I learned to listen to God's voice for instructions. Every morning I would wake up and ask the Lord to show me what He wanted me to do. It might be that I was to invite my husband home for lunch and make love to him. This is embarrassing, but I couldn't even love my husband the way I wanted, because I didn't have the strength. When you're in good health it's easy to take life for granted, but when you lack the strength to do anything, then dependence on the Lord becomes a necessity. Some days I would crawl down the stairs to do the laundry and have to stay there until evening when my husband could come home and help me back up the stairs. For months and months I was limited to crawling . . . so I was literally on my hands and knees before the Lord. I continue to be dependent on the Lord and others.

I haven't given up hope that someday I will be better. Every day I pray for God's healing. But in the midst of this situation I have come to accept my limitations. For a person who thought she could live outside of boundaries, this is a big step. God has helped me reset my priorities. I've also learned to appreciate and receive from my family. I don't think I could have coped with this illness had it not been for the most wonderful husband in the world, Daniel. My children have loved and served me. They have learned to clean the house, cook, do laundry, and be more self-sufficient. I believe they are better people for all the responsibilities they've shouldered. If I ever do get my health back, you can be assured, I'll never take feeling well again for granted. Yes, I never counted on this one.

Lost and Found!

Sharon never thought her life would turn out in such a way. Raised in an alcoholic, rage-a-holic family, Sharon found the easiest way out was to marry the first stable guy she met.

So at nineteen she married "good old reliable" Fred. Seventeen years and two children later, Sharon grew more and more dissatisfied with her life, but especially with steady Fred. What had appealed to her as solid and secure, now felt ice-cold and boringly predictable. Sharon wanted out of the marriage. "When is it going to be my turn?" she thought. "There's got to be more out there than what I've got."

Little did Sharon know how many times she would regret leaving her husband and children to pursue "her" life. She didn't know how good she had it.

Sharon said, "I've spent thousands of dollars with therapists through the years trying to overcome the enormous guilt of leaving my children."

Today, four divorces and five marriages later, she admits, "I never counted on this."

However, after years of aimless wondering and selfish indulgences, Sharon has found what she was looking for all along:

All my life, I've tried to find someone who would love

me. The rejection and abuse I experienced from my mother and father left me with a hole in my heart that could not be filled. But five years ago, after searching everywhere from the occult to all manner of perverse living, I finally found someone who would accept me, love me, cherish and keep me. I finally found Jesus.

Do I regret being married and divorced so many times? Do I loathe the fact that I left my children and lived only for self? I would give anything to undo the harm I've done to those I love, but I can't. Of course, I know I have to live with the consequences of my sin, but God's grace has proven sufficient for me. Christ has forgiven me, and my life is completely different.

Whether anyone else accepts it or not, I know I am a new creation in Christ. When God sees me, He doesn't see me as a divorced woman who has messed up more times than I'm comfortable admitting, but instead God sees the righteousness of Christ. The day I converted to Christ everything changed. The way I thought changed, my values changed, my morals changed. It was wonderful. Jesus has healed my wounded heart, given me the power to forgive my parents, helped me secure the forgiveness from those I have hurt, and has cleansed my life. I am not the same person I was, thank God.

Jesus has shown me that no matter what I've done, Christ is not only the answer to my life, He is the only *question*!

Victim or Victor?

I have always loved the poem *The Tapestry*, even though it makes me uncomfortable. If anyone hates pain and suffering, it's me. I'm a big baby when I contract even a simple cold. I complain to every store clerk and bag boy, giving full disclosure of persistent symptoms and cost of prescriptions. I never suffer alone or in silence. Nonetheless, suffering, great and small (whether it's great or small depends on whether I'm the one doing the suffering), is a part of our lives. Keeping in mind that God is in control and has a purpose for our lives may make the difference between being a victim or a victor.

The Tapestry[1]

My life is but a weaving between my Lord and me;
I cannot choose the colors, He worketh steadily.
Ofttimes, He weaveth sorrow, and I in foolish pride
Forget that He seeth the upper, and I the underside.

Not 'til the loom is silent, and the shutters cease to fly,
Shall God unroll the canvas and explain the reason why.
The dark threads are as needful in the weaver's skillful hand
As the threads of gold and silver in the pattern He has
    planned.

Stop! Read this poem again. In these simple words the difficult truths of life are revealed.

Nothing to Lose; Everything to Gain!

The Widow of Nain had lost everything (Luke 7:11–18). Having already experienced the death of her husband, she was on her way out of the city to bury her only son when she met Jesus.

This woman now was alone. With no husband or son to provide a living for her, she must have been feeling the panic of abandonment. Seeing the sadness of the widow and being moved by compassion, Jesus said to her, "Do not weep." He then touched the coffin and told the boy to "arise." Jesus gave the boy back to his mother. Is it any wonder that all who witnessed this miracle began to glorify God?

Whenever Jesus arrives on the scene, things begin to happen. Sometimes the miracle is experienced when God makes everything all better. When a child miraculously recovers, a laboratory test comes back negative, an accident is averted, or a financial situation turned around, we joyfully and vocally praise God.

However, the same God who is able to snatch us from disaster will also carry us through the Valley of the Shadow of Death. Every story doesn't turn out the way we want it to, but God's grace is sufficient in times of heartache and heartbreak.

I love the words to this old hymn, which remind us of God's love for us in times of trouble.

---

[1]A. Naismith, *2400 Scripture Outlines, Anecdotes, Notes and Quotes* (Grand Rapids, Mich.: Baker Book House, 1963).

He giveth more grace when the burdens grow greater;
He sendeth more strength when the labors increase;
To added affliction He addeth His mercy,
To multiplied trials, His multiplied peace.

When we have exhausted our store of endurance,
When our strength has failed ere the day is half done,
When we reach the end of our hoarded resources,
Our Father's full giving is only begun.

His love has no limits, His grace has no measure,
His power has no boundary known unto men,
For out of His infinite riches in Jesus
He giveth, and giveth, and giveth again.[2]

James 5:13–16 gives instruction to those who are experiencing difficult times. "Is any among you suffering? Let him pray.
Is any cheerful? Let him sing praises. Is anyone among you sick?
Let him call for the elders of the church, and let them pray over
him, anointing him with oil in the name of the Lord."

Pastor Jack Hayford has pointed out that somehow, through
the years, we have misinterpreted the instructions given in this
passage. In verse thirteen, James speaks to those who are *suffering*. (The Greek word *kakopathei* indicates any distress, suffering of hardships, or any trouble, other than sickness.) This suffering person is told to pray.

I heard of one pastor who told individuals seeking his counsel that he would talk to them only after they had prayed diligently for two weeks concerning their problem. If they still
needed help, then and only then would he discuss their situation. That pastor was following the instruction given by James.
Today when we have a problem, we are often encouraged to call
on the elders of the church (or a counselor of some type) and
ask *them* to pray, instead of our taking the situation to the Lord
first.

Many times we are timid about taking our problems to the
Lord because we don't know *how* to pray, and we've learned to
rely on others to do our praying for us. Ask God to help you
pray and He will guide you. Here are some scriptural guidelines
to keep in mind as you talk with the Lord.

---

[2]Annie Johnson Flint and Hubert Mitchell, 1941.

Pray
to the Father (John 16:23)
in the name of Jesus (John 14:12–15)
by the Holy Spirit (Romans 8:26)
in harmony with the Word of God (John 15:7)
in faith, nothing doubting (James 1:6)
with praise for the answer (Philippians 4:6).

James goes on to speak to those who are cheerful. "Is any cheerful? Let him sing praises." It is so unfair to expect those who are suffering to sing praises. It is truly a burden when you're struggling through a problem and other Christians are urging you to be cheerful and happy. There will come a time when the songs of praise will spring forth, but during times of sorrow, let those who weep, weep in peace. There is a time and purpose for everything. There is a time to laugh and a time to weep (Ecclesiastes 3:4). We should not put pressure on suffering Christians to perform and pretend to be happy when their hearts are breaking. Singing praises is something God brings forth, not other prodding Christians. We need to give those who are suffering a break—take the pressure off of them, pray for them, and leave them alone.

"Is anyone among you sick?" Verse fourteen continues, "Let him call for the elders of the church." Again, we seem to get these things mixed up. We tell a person who is sick to pray, and we tell a person who is suffering to call on the elders of the church.

Perhaps one reason the Scriptures instruct the sick to call for the elders is to bring light to the situation. (Notice here, the elders are not the ones to go seeking the sick; it's the responsibility of the sick to do the calling.) So many people will suffer illness silently, and the illness gets worse. Isolation can be as debilitating as the illness itself. Calling on others to assist can be part of the healing process.

"Don't Be Afraid; It Is I!"

Jesus sent the disciples to the other side of the Sea of Galilee so He could go to the mountains and pray. While the disciples were sailing across the sea, a violent storm unexpectedly arose. When they started their trip they had never counted on getting into a situation where their lives would be in jeopardy.

It was during the fourth watch that Jesus came to them in the midst of the storm. The fourth watch was between the hours of 3:00 A.M. and 6:00 A.M. If you've ever been in the hospital with an ill loved one, then you know those hours seem like an eternity.

During the last few hours of my niece's struggle with cystic fibrosis, our family was gathered together with my brother. One night I was talking to a nurse who worked on the floor where the terminally ill children spent their final hours. She told me, "If a patient is going to die, it will usually be during those late night or early morning hours. If they can stay alive until the sun comes up in the morning, it seems to give everyone a new start. There's just something about making it through those darkest hours."

It was no mistake that Jesus came to the disciples during the darkest, most lonely hours of the night. When they saw Him coming, walking on the water, they thought He was a ghost. Jesus spoke simple words to them that changed the outcome of *their* storm. He said, "Take courage; don't be afraid. It is I."

This is the same courage from which we must draw in the bleakness of our lives. When sad, terrible things happen to us, we must look for Jesus coming to us in the darkest time, walking through the storm, comforting us with the words, "Don't be afraid, I'm here."

What simple words of comfort: "I'm here." In the same way Jesus spoke to the disciples, He speaks to us. He doesn't tell us that there is no storm, but He *does* tell us that there is no danger . . . and to be courageous, for we are not alone.

Do bad things happen to us? Yes. Do people we love leave us and hurt us? Yes. Do we wrong those who love us? Yes. What is it, then, that keeps us from dying of fear? How do we endure the relentless waves of grief and pain? We look for Jesus coming to us. Sometimes He stills the storm and makes the bad go away. But sometimes He walks right through the middle of it, and even asks us to get out of the boat and walk the path of suffering with Him. Our only hope for surviving the blows of life is to take courage in knowing that He is there with us.

We cannot control the sad things that happen to us. That's not our responsibility, but our willingness to place our hand in His and walk the path of suffering will bring us ultimately to a deeper knowledge of Him and His goodness.

But whatever was to my profit I now consider loss for the sake of Christ. What is more, I consider everything a loss compared to the surpassing greatness of knowing Christ Jesus our Lord, for whose sake I have lost all things. I consider them rubbish, that I may gain Christ and be found in him, not having a righteousness of my own that comes from the law, but that which is through faith in Christ—the righteousness that comes from God and is by faith. I want to know Christ and the power of his resurrection and the fellowship of sharing in his sufferings, becoming like him in his death, and so somehow, to attain to the resurrection from the dead. (Philippians 3:7–11, NIV)

I consider that our present sufferings are not worth comparing with the glory that will be revealed in us. (Romans 8:18, NIV)

10

Can Worth Be
Weighed on a Bathroom Scale?

I did it again! I said I wasn't going to do it, but I did it anyway. I purchased another book about losing weight and how to keep it off, forever. . . . Yeah, right! As I make this confession, I realize that this obsession with weight loss, workout videos, and exercise equipment is boring me to death.

If the escalating sales of such books and gimmicks are any indication, then I am comforted (and appalled!) to know I am not the only obsessed, weight-conscious "sucker" out there. Any celebrity who has maintained weight loss for more than twenty-four hours has a book proclaiming, "I'll never be fat again!"

The world watched as talk show host Oprah Winfrey pulled a wagon filled with sixty-seven pounds of fat on stage during one of her television broadcasts. I tearfully cheered her, along with every other skinny-wannabe, as she announced the end to her weight problems. Honestly, I wanted her to be thin forever. Sadly, though, millions watched as her lost pounds eventually returned and the inches piled back on. Disappointed and disillusioned, a few months later Oprah announced to the listening world, "I'll never diet again!"

Finding peace with her size seemed more sane than the endless gain/lose cycle she had followed in the past. However, that "peace with herself and her size" was short-lived. She has once again lost the weight, and this time she has announced that she has found the "real answer" to her weight problem. She is succeeding this time to keep a trim figure through personal attitude adjustments, by eating only low-fat, high-fiber foods (she has a professional cook who prepares her meals), and by working out hours every day (she has a full-time personal trainer as well). I am happy for her success, but how many of us have the same resources to devote to staying slim?

The obsession with our weight and appearance is not just a peculiarity to the Hollywood jet set. Women in all stations of life seem to be judged according to a standard of beauty that is extremely difficult to attain, and at times infeasible to maintain. To escape the message that links our worth with our weight, and our value to our volume, is most difficult. It's unfortunate that how we look has become much more the focus than who we are. A better use of energy would be for us to recognize the illusion of beauty for what it is. Proverbs 31:30 says, "Charm is deceitful and beauty is vain, but a woman who fears the Lord, she shall be praised." Keeping that godly perspective on a daily basis ought to be our challenge.

The Illusion of Beauty

Standing in the grocery line, innocently waiting to check out my items, I am once again hammered by the barrage of magazine covers. Looking at me from the glossy pages are perfectly proportioned, immaculately groomed, and knock-dead gorgeous women. And the headlines promise that I too can lose ten pounds in two days. (It's uncanny how they always know that I need to lose ten pounds!) The glamorous women look so together, so happy, yet so totally plastic. How do they achieve and maintain such superb beauty and shape?

While reading the newspaper the other day, I found out how one notorious beauty comes by her great looks. The article was about Princess Diana of Wales. It seems that hubby, Charles, was a might miffed at his princess. Being a natural beauty can be quite expensive, and Charles was less than enthusiastic about footing the bill. Somehow, I think Steve might have a problem if every *week* I spent $2,642.31 for clothes, $270.58 on hair (and I thought those highlights were natural), and $642.69 on various beauty treatments. The annual expenses were $240,700 and that's just the expenses Charles had to pay; that doesn't count any money Princess Di spent of her own. Honestly, any one of us could look grand if we had a royal expense account like Princess Di, could afford an in-house chef like Oprah Winfrey, or were married to our own plastic surgeon like Victoria Principal! (Is it face cream that took away Victoria's wrinkles and gave her such a great chest?)

USA Today printed the third annual "Nip and Tuck" Awards, which appeared in *Longevity* magazine. Karyn Repinski, the magazine's beauty editor, reported, "When we interviewed celebrities on how they stayed so young, nobody ever owned up to surgery, and lots of times it was so apparent. We decided to level the playing field and take a closer look so readers wouldn't get discouraged as to why they didn't look that good."

The magazine revealed that such celebrities as Bette Midler, Sharon Stone, Cindy Crawford, Tina Turner, Michelle Pfeiffer, Demi Moore, Shannen Doherty, Jennifer Grey, Tori Spelling, Goldie Hawn, Heather Locklear, and Victoria Principal have been "perfected" through cosmetic surgery. Other stories have pointed to nips and tucks, and crops and chops, performed on Roseanne, Melissa Gilbert, Cher, and Elizabeth Taylor. Dolly Parton admits, "Yes, I have had cosmetic surgery. . . . It's not only a right, but an obligation for a woman, especially a woman in the public eye, to look as good as she can." Some of Dolly's "improvements" were on her breasts (I would never have guessed), waist (I thought as much), buttocks (now that's an idea worth looking into), and multiple facial procedures (ouch!). It is tragic when regular women, like you and me, think we can look like these celebrity women merely through diet and exercise.

The American Academy of Cosmetic Surgery reported, "Although estimates vary, at least 150,000 women a year in the United States have breast implant surgery. . . . Eighty percent are for nonmedical reasons, most often to enlarge the breast. The only cosmetic surgery more frequently performed than breast augmentation is liposuction [to siphon away body fat]."[1]

---

[1]Lena Williams, "Women and Self-Image: Seeing Through a Glass Darkly," *The Tennessean*, February 9, 1994.

Think of the insanity! Women electively having complicated, irreversible (not to mention expensive) surgical alterations just to have bigger breasts, a flatter stomach, and thinner hips and thighs.

Why do we let ourselves get jerked around by the deceptions of the TV, modeling, and movie industries, by comparing ourselves with these women who have the resources to fix anything they want to surgically, as well as the time and money to dedicate their lives to their appearance? Not only that, but these women also have access to incredible photographic technology, which can work all sorts of wonders.

I've had firsthand experience with this modern technology. It was during the photo session for our "Between the Two of Them" CD cover that I learned just why these women look flawless. Steve was unhappy with the way his front teeth looked in the picture. So with computer-generated technology, they took a tooth from my mouth and put it in his. They also, I'll admit, removed a mole and a few wrinkles from my face. I learned from that experience that the pictures on the covers of the magazines that haunt me at the grocery checkout line are not honest portrayals of the women I am daily enticed to look like.

According to Jennifer Brenner, a professor of psychology at Brandeis University, "Female models are 9 percent taller and 16 percent thinner than average women, an unrealistic ideal of beauty for women to emulate. . . . We should accept these women as [being] unique, or put forth an ideal image of women which is more compatible with the average female body." And what is the size of the average American woman? One-third of American women are size 14 and above.[2]

Dr. Joyce Brothers said, in an article for *Reader's Digest*, "What Men Don't Understand About Women": "Despite decades of feminism, women get the message that it still pays to be beautiful, just as in the days of fairy tales. With all the pressure to be young and attractive, even the most beautiful women can feel that they come up short, and go to pieces when they gain a few pounds or notice a few wrinkles."[3]

---

[2]Ibid.
[3]Dr. Joyce Brothers, "What Men Don't Understand About Women," *Reader's Digest* (July 1994).

Stop Blaming!

Knowing the truth and living according to that truth may be easier said than done. Living in a world that quickly judges women according to their appearance—specifically, weight and conditioning—makes it hard to mentally adjust. If we are physically unfit, it's easy to feel like a misfit. Blaming others can be a way of dealing with those feelings. Blaming is not only unfair, it is nonproductive. Listen to some of the comments I've heard from women who are struggling with the issue of dealing with weight and worth, value and volume.

Jennifer

"If I didn't work outside the home I'd be able to control my weight. My job is so stressful it's hard for me to concentrate on everything plus watch my diet. The candy machine, co-workers bringing in donuts every morning, and constantly being offered food makes it impossible for me to diet. If I didn't have to work I could be involved in an exercise program and have time to plan a healthy menu. There's no time to exercise with my schedule. I get up as early as I can, and when I come home there's too many other things that have to be done. There's simply no time for me. No, I'm convinced, working this job is why I can't get my weight under control."

Tamara

"If I wasn't home all day with my children I'd be able to lose weight. There's no way I can diet when I'm fixing food for the children all day, passing out cookies and Kool-Aid; there's no way I can keep from eating these things. So much of my life is doing things I don't want to do. Mentally, I can't handle not being able to eat what I want. If I worked outside the home, I'd have more control of my environment. I could take a walk at noon and pack my lunch. As it is, there's no way I can stay on a food program when I spend ten hours a day in the kitchen. I can't even exercise. Every time I get down on the floor to do exercises, the kids think I want to play and they tackle me. As long as I'm home, there's no hope of losing weight."

Lynn

"If I had a more supportive family I'd be able to lose this weight. Every time I start to get a grip on my eating and see some progress in losing weight, my husband brings home a double-meat, double-cheese, deep-dish pizza. Why does he do that? He knows I can't resist pizza! He sabotages me every time I start to do well. Maybe my husband thinks I'll leave him if I lose weight. I need a family that will encourage me, instead of complaining because I can't go eat at our favorite Mexican restaurant. I'm convinced I could lose weight if I had a different family."

The sentiments expressed by these three women are understandable complaints. There's some truth in each statement, for obviously our circumstances can make life more difficult. But ultimately no one pries our mouths open and makes us eat anything we don't want. When we find ourselves saying, "No, thank you. I wish I could have a chocolate donut, but I can't. I'm on a diet," we are setting ourselves up for failure. Depriving ourselves may work for a while, but in the long run our negative attitudes will defeat our efforts. We should instead adopt the attitude of, "I can eat anything I want, but I choose not to eat the donut." We need to put the responsibility for controlling ourselves back into our own hands.

Stop Obsessing!

There's a balance to be found in achieving and maintaining an acceptable discipline for our bodies. Somewhere beyond this crazy obsession is the place of true freedom. Being healthy and holy should be the goal of every Christian woman.

Of course, there's nothing wrong with wanting to have a healthy, toned body. Unfortunately, we must face the fact that we live in a world where there's little tolerance for a body that is overweight and out of shape. Nonetheless, the desire to work on a healthy, disciplined lifestyle of eating right foods and exercising should be motivated by caring for God's temple, as well as looking and feeling our best. It's when we think that how we look has *anything* to do with *who we are*, that we set ourselves up for a "striving after wind." (See Ecclesiastes 1:17.)

There is no happiness to be found in thinness for thinness'

sake. Just ask a person suffering from the life-threatening disease of anorexia nervosa, where strict dieting crosses over into self-inflicted, suicidal starvation. Ask them, "When is thin, thin enough?" The most common answer the person with anorexia gives is, "Just a little thinner."

When "thin" becomes the focus, rather than a reasonable weight maintenance and a strong, healthy body, then the results can be both disastrous and ultimately deadly.

Having achieved her goal weight and toned her body, Kathy was forced to ask herself the question, "When am I going to enjoy this hard-earned achievement?" When Kathy's husband came in and invited her out to dinner at their favorite steak house, she turned him down. She said she couldn't go out to eat because she might regain some weight. So, they'd have to eat at home. When a girl friend asked her to go out for an "all-you-can-eat" seafood night at a terrific restaurant, she had to decline. "I can't risk going to that restaurant. I love the food too much; I might overeat." Kathy was limiting her life simply to maintain a certain number on the scale. How sad that we would miss spending time with family or friends because of weight.

The truth is, we can be healthy, happy, and holy without being a size 4, 6, or 8. We can enjoy being with our friends and family without being controlled by what we can and cannot eat.

Weight obsession is a prison. Freedom is not found in giving up and eating a pound of fudge. Freedom is found in both disciplining our bodies and renewing our minds. It's obvious that 1 Corinthians 9:27 does not reflect a lax attitude about physical discipline. "Like an athlete I punish my body, treating it roughly, training it to do what it should, not what it wants to. Otherwise I fear that after enlisting others for the race, I myself might be declared unfit and ordered to stand aside" (TLB).

Feeding our bodies good, healthy foods is a reasonable responsibility. But too easily, moderate discipline can cross the line and fall into a self-centered attitude. Dieting can be one of the most self-absorbed activities there are. Every decision is based on where and what *I* can eat.

Too much needed energy is used up with body obsession. It's time to stop blaming others for our situation and take responsibility for our own actions. We need to stop this manic pursuit of thinness and simply seek a healthy body and mind.

What? Men and Women are Different?

In her book *Outsmarting the Female Fat Cell*, Debra Waterhouse explains the dilemma women face when it comes to controlling their weight.[4]

> I came to realize the female fat cell is different from the male fat cell, which makes weight loss tougher for women than for men.
>
> The storage of fat is called *lipogenesis* ("lipo" means fat; "genesis" means formation). The release of fat is called lipolysis ("lysis" means breakdown). The enzymes that help store fat are lipogenic enzymes; the enzymes that help release fat are lipolytic enzymes. The difference between male and female fat cells lies in the enzyme systems and the size of the fat cells. . . . Women have more lipogenic enzymes for the storage of fat. . . . Men have more lipolytic enzymes for the release of fat and, therefore, smaller fat cells. . . . Women store fat quickly and lose it slowly; men store fat slowly and lose it quickly.
>
> The male sex hormone, testosterone, activates the lipolytic enzymes for the speedy release of fat. . . . Estrogen concentrates its storing effort in the buttocks, hips and thighs. (This is why the average woman has a size 8 top and a size 12 bottom.)

Fearfully and Wonderfully Made!

Is it not strange how we fight against our bodies? This is a result of living in a culture that has created an unnatural and unrealistic expectation of appearance. There was a time in history when a size 12, 14, or 16 were model sizes. That is not the case anymore. Our culture instead values those women who starve themselves into a state of poor health, who deny themselves food to the point where their bodies do not resemble the soft, rounded, feminine bodies of our foremothers, but the lean, hard, sinewy bodies of our forefathers.

As Christian women, we are faced with a choice. Do we reject the genetic makeup of our feminine bodies, or do we strive to adapt to this modern culture of thinner and leaner is better? God

---

[4]Debra Waterhouse, *Outsmarting the Female Fat Cell* (New York: Warner Books, 1994).

says we are "fearfully and wonderfully made" (Psalm 139:14). When we realize all that has gone into making us, then perhaps we can value ourselves beyond the measurement of the bathroom scale. Instead of worshiping the creation, we must turn our worship to the Creator. (See Romans 1:22–23.)

Why the undue pressure for women, who are physically and genetically predisposed to carrying more body fat than men, to be ultra-thin? Nothing illustrates a woman's wonderfully made body more than when we take a look at its genetic makeup. There is a built-in survival mechanism in our bodies that is triggered when food is withheld. During times of famine, the people who survived were the ones who had a reserve of fat in their bodies, and the ones whose bodies were the best at conserving the fat they ingested. A woman's body needed more fat than a man's just in case she was pregnant. The fat-storing backup system was designed to protect the human race from extinction. In our modern world, sometimes the only time an already overweight woman is given permission to feel good about her body is during pregnancy.

I believe the pressure on women to be rail thin is at best a subconscious attitude, and at worst a blatant attack on, and devaluing of, motherhood. The soft, rounded bodies of our foremothers were designed to birth children, breast-feed them, and nurture them throughout childhood. Currently, the trend is for women to have thin, muscle-bound, hard bodies with minimal body fat.

Look at the models who are presented as the ultimate in great looks. They are razor thin, no waists, no hips—everything about them denies feminine softness. (And for those thin models with unnaturally large breasts, we get the message that the sole purpose of the female body is to be sexually stimulating.) I remember one day in my "non-thin" days, Nathan was sitting on my lap and he said, "Oh, Mommy, I love to sit on your lap. It's so nice and squashy." I've been given compliments that I've enjoyed more, but to a child, a nice cushioned lap is more comfortable than one on which, if you're not careful, you might cut yourself on a bone.

God instituted the differences in the way men and women store energy. Men did not need as much fat, because they did not need to potentially feed another human life. When women complain that they lose weight slowly and gain it back quickly, they are right. A woman's body does not readily release fat, because she might need it for reproduction. Instead of crying "foul" and resenting the way our bodies work, we need to change our expectation and cry out, "Yes, I agree, I am fearfully and wonderfully made. God does all things right."

Our bodies consist of various chemicals: iron, sugar, salt, carbon, iodine, phosphorus, lime, calcium, and other trace minerals. The monetary value of our bodies would be around ninety-eight cents. However, God has invested much more in us. Our bodies contain 263 bones, 600 muscles, 970 miles of blood vessels, and 400 taste buds on the tongue. We have 20,000 hairs in our ears to conduct sound. We also have forty pounds of jaw pressure; 10,000,000 nerves and branches; 3,500 sweat tubes to each square inch of skin; 20,000,000 openings that suck food as it goes through the intestines; 600,000,000 air cells in our lungs that inhale 2,400 gallons of air daily; and a telephone system that relates to the brain instantly any known sound, taste, sight, touch, or smell. The heart beats 4,200 times an hour and pumps twelve tons of blood daily.[5]

Does this sound like a machine that should be denied food, water, or exercise? God has made us in such a wonderful and fearful way, why would we abuse our bodies with insufficient food, inadequate foods ("Here, have a donut and a cup of coffee"), or too much food? No! We must treat our bodies with the love and respect they deserve, because of the One who created us. First Corinthians 6:12 and 19 says, "Everything is permissible for me, but not everything is beneficial. Everything is permissible for me, but I will not be mastered by anything. . . . Do you not know that your body is the temple of the Holy Spirit, who is in you and whom you have received from God?" (NIV).

We are not to be mastered by the temptation, on one hand, to gobble up the chocolate cheesecake, nor on the other hand, controlled by the goal of slipping into a pair of size six blue jeans. Our only master should be our holy God. How can we follow Him when our eyes are firmly fixed on our thighs?

Christ-Esteem, Not Self-Esteem!

One day while Heidi and I were walking in the mall, Heidi spotted a group of young girls her age. She didn't know the

---

[5]Finis Jennings Dake, *Dake's Annotated Bible* (Lawrenceville, Ga.: Dake Bible Sales, Inc., 1963).

girls, and yet she seemed to feel very uncomfortable. I said, "Heidi, what's wrong? Do you know those girls?" She looked up at me in complete sincerity and said, "No, I don't know them, but they think I'm fat."

How sad that Heidi was projecting her own self-conscious feelings onto total strangers. Heidi had a problem, but it wasn't low self-esteem. Her problem was thinking too much about "self." Because she was uncomfortable with her appearance and this was on her mind constantly, she thought everyone else was consumed with it as well.

Even though Heidi was only ten years old, we started making better food choices and taking walks together. Throughout that summer Heidi lost fifteen pounds. Along with the exercise and food program, we also talked about the wrongness of an over-concentration on SELF. A poor attitude toward one's self is not low "self-esteem," it is low "Christ-esteem." The very fact that self is the center of thought and attention should indicate a sin problem. Our goal in life should be to serve Christ before serving ourself and others. Feeling good about ourselves should never be our focus. This search for self-esteem and building up of one's self may be the American way, but it's not God's way.

Nowhere in all of the Bible do I find a model for building up or bolstering the SELF. In fact, the very opposite approach to life is what I find. In Philippians 3, Paul wrote, "If anyone else thinks he has reasons to put confidence in the flesh, I have more: circumcised on the eighth day, of the people of Israel, of the tribe of Benjamin, a Hebrew of Hebrews, in regard to the law, a Pharisee; as for zeal, persecuting the church; as for legalistic righteousness, faultless. But whatever was to my profit I now consider loss for the sake of Christ" (vv. 4–7, NIV). After delineating his impressive credentials, Paul continued by saying, "But whatever things *were gain to me*, those things I have counted as *loss for the sake of Christ.* More than that, I count all things to be loss in view of the surpassing value of knowing Christ Jesus my Lord, for whom I have suffered the loss of all things, and count them but rubbish" (vv. 7–8). (The King James Version calls Paul's wonderful accomplishments "dung," or "manure.")

After Paul compared who he was according to his accomplishment, and who he was in regards to his relationship with Christ, there was only one conclusion. He identified himself with Christ, and Christ alone. In like manner, whether our list of "who we are and what we've done" can stand up to Paul's accomplishments is immaterial. Anything and everything is "manure" when placed alongside of who we are in Christ. If Christ is our identity, there is no room left for self.

Whenever we seek as our identity and worth (self-esteem) *anything* other than our relationship with Jesus Christ and who we are in Him, then whatever is in His place is an idol. That idol may be our family name, good looks, great body, intellect, professional successes, political persuasion, or church affiliation.

When Bethany House Publishers released our first book, *Married Lovers, Married Friends*, Steve and I were invited to the CBA (Christian Booksellers Association) convention. We were given our badges to wear that would admit us onto the convention floor. In big, black, bold letters under our name was the word AUTHOR.

All the years before when we'd attended the CBA, we were with the music division. The difference between being identified as AUTHOR versus ARTIST was astounding. With the word "author" under our names, we were treated with much more respect. It was assumed, rightly or not, that if we were authors, we possessed some measure of intelligence. This was contrasted with the music title of "artist," where the assumption is made that you lack moral and intellectual capacity.

Reflecting back on this situation, I see how easily I let the title of "author" give me identity and allowed me to feed into the world of self-importance. Actually, the only title worn at the convention should have been SERVANTS OF THE MOST HIGH GOD. Regardless of the particular function we may perform, serving God is where it begins and ends.

John the Baptist did not boast his position in the Kingdom. When the Pharisees came to him and inquired if he was "somebody" (John 1:19–24), his response was clear. He did not base his identity on his ministry, nor his loyal following, nor his accomplishments (nowhere would you find in his publicity packet, "I baptized the Messiah!"), but his identity was based on his relationship with Jesus. After all was said and done, John the Baptist concluded in John 3:30, "He must increase, but I must decrease."

In Matthew 16:24, Jesus said, "If any man will come after me, let him deny himself, and take up his cross and follow me" (KJV). This is a little different from the modern-day implication,

"Take up your throne and follow me."

Colossians 2:6–10 leaves no room for us to wonder where we should derive our identity and worth. "As you therefore have received Christ Jesus the Lord, so walk in Him, having been firmly rooted and now being built up in Him and established in your faith, just as you were instructed, and overflowing with gratitude. See to it that no one takes you captive through philosophy and empty deception, according to the tradition of men, according to the elementary principles of the world, rather than according to Christ. For in Him . . . you have been made complete."

We are complete in Christ. It is Christ alone. Our problem is not low self-esteem; our problem is low Christ-esteem. Don't worry about self; self always gets enough attention.

Valuable or Valued

I had spoken at a ladies luncheon. As I was packing up, a gentleman who was on staff at the church came to ask me for a favor. He explained that his wife had looked forward to the luncheon and had planned on coming that day, but because of her health, she was unable to attend. He asked if I would mind stopping by his house on the way out of town to say hello to her. I agreed. As we entered the front door he told me a little of their story.

They had married about fifteen years earlier. I looked at their wedding pictures as he told me of their first year together. She was strikingly beautiful. Tall, slender with long chestnut brown hair. They were indeed a handsome couple. Life went on as expected until one day she fell down. The falls became more frequent as she realized she was losing strength in her legs. A trip to the doctor sadly revealed a fast-growing form of multiple sclerosis. This terrible disease viciously attacked her nervous system, leaving her in a wheelchair.

By the time I saw her, I was unprepared for the scene. We entered the bedroom and there she lay, her body twisted and deformed. Gone were the long, flowing locks of brown hair. Instead she wore a manageable short, cropped style more suitable for the years she had spent in bed. The woman in the bed bore no resemblance to the beauty queen in the wedding pictures, yet I witnessed something unexpected as we walked into her room. I glanced up at the husband. What I saw nearly made me blush. I was standing in the presence of two people who were obviously in love. The way this man looked at his wife, and the way she teasingly flirted with him was so personal and deeply intimate I felt honored, yet somewhat intrusive, to have shared that moment. As I stood there in the room I realized why this seemed so special. Without question, I was observing true love. The kind of love without conditions. He loved her, not for what she could give him—for obviously she was more than limited in her ability to express her love—but he loved her because she belonged to him. This couple had found what the whole world is looking for. While the rest of this crazy, sexually frustrated, morally perverse society is bounding from one encounter to another, true love is found in the privilege of belonging.

In the eyes of the world, this poor, disfigured woman could have been seen as one who had nothing to contribute to her family or society. But through the eyes of love all of that changed, and I saw a woman of tremendous value.

So it is that we all are paralyzed and twisted in one way or another. But it's in our belonging to Christ, who loves us unconditionally, that gives us our ultimate worth.

Looking for Help in All the Right Places—Finally!

Could any woman ever have felt worse about her body than the woman in Mark 5:25–34. This poor Israelite woman had suffered for twelve years with a constant menstrual flow. According to the Levitical law she was considered unclean—unworthy of even being touched. Anywhere she sat was deemed unclean (Leviticus 15:20). Anyone who touched her was unclean (Leviticus 15:19). Anyone who touched anything that she had touched was unclean and had to go through a series of bathing rituals to rid themselves of the uncleanliness (Leviticus 15:27). By law, this woman was a nuisance, a person of diminished value.

For twelve years she had not only suffered in her body, but she was shunned by society. She had become easy prey for the physicians who took her money and yet gave her no remedy for her plague. Instead of helping her, they made the situation even worse (Mark 5:26).

Things seemed utterly hopeless, and humanly speaking they were. Here was a woman in a desperate situation. She had tried all human remedies. She had spent all her human resources. What was she to do? Her only hope began when (in verse 27) "she heard of Jesus." Determined to touch Jesus, she pressed through the crowd. What courage, what faith this poor woman displayed! Reaching out to touch Jesus meant opening herself to ridicule. She also risked the scorn of Jesus and His disciples, for by touching Him, she contaminated Jesus with her "uncleanness." Yet, driven by her enormous need, she reached out to Jesus. Instantly, we are told, she was healed of the plague that had nearly destroyed her life.

Jesus, recognizing "the touch of faith," asked for her to come forward. Trembling and fearful, knowing what she had done, she came to Him, fell down at His feet, and made her confession before Him for all to hear.

When Jesus looked at that broken, pitiful woman, He did not see what everyone else saw. He saw a woman of worth because she was a woman of faith. He deemed her worthy of the healing power that flowed from Him to her. She was worthy to be called "daughter." She was worthy to be sent on her way whole in body and spirit to live in peace.

This woman whom the religious people had called "unclean," whom family, friends, and neighbors had shunned, and whom the professionals had robbed of money and dignity, Jesus called "daughter."

Where is our worth? Is it in the way we look, where we live, how we dress, and who on earth we know? Absolutely not! Our worth—body and soul—is found in our desperate pursuit of Christ, reaching out to Him for help, and with humility being received as His child.

The condition or appearance of our bodies has nothing to do with our value. Our value was set when God deemed us worthy of the life of His Son. As women, we must somehow accept the fact that our value to God has absolutely nothing to do with how we look. This old body is just a cardboard box that houses the Hope Diamond, for our hope is in Christ. The value is not in the packaging, but in the contents. It's high time we start polishing the diamond, instead of weighing the box.

11

Refueled and Refreshed

It is often said "one man's junk is another man's (or in my case, woman's) treasure." I find this to be most true on days when I tackle the job of straightening the miscellaneous "treasure" on top of Steve's dresser. (I'm not sure why I feel compelled to tidy up those little scraps of paper, loose change, receipts, pens, keys, buttons, and a million other little things of Steve's, when I know that three months from now I'll be asked what I did with that torn piece of yellow paper that had something really important on it . . . like a song idea or lyrics). On this particular day, I had discovered a long-forgotten jar of coins buried under a stack of baseball caps. I found some coin wrappers and started wrapping. Gathering momentum, I decided to gather and wrap all of the loose change around the house.

By the time the morning was over, I had found and wrapped $246.00 worth of coins! When I had started my coin wrapping project, there didn't appear to be that much money; mostly pennies, nickels and dimes, with a few quarters. But when all of the coins were put together, they amounted to something rather substantial.

To my pleasant surprise, Steve's mess was of more value than I had anticipated. This can be said of other areas in our lives. Too many of us feel overdrawn and shortchanged when it comes to fulfilling the many responsibilities we face each day. But even though we may not have vast amounts of time and energy, we can look at the "pennies, nickels, and dimes" hidden in our day and find resources that we may have overlooked or discarded as not having much value.

Where Does My Help Come From?

Psalm 121:1–2 says, "I lift up my eyes to the hills—where does my help come from? My help comes from the Lord, the Maker of heaven and earth" (NIV). We may find the beauty of nature absolutely invigorating. We may feel a sense of resurgence when we can get away and enjoy the great outdoors. But the truth remains, our help doesn't come from God's creation, it comes from the Creator himself. God has provided us with a variety of resources from which we can derive the necessary fuel and refreshment to make it through any of life's situations.

Refueled Through the Word of God

Each morning, the Israelites did as God had instructed them and gathered the manna, which He provided as their daily source of "fuel." Only when consumed fresh (it could not be stored) did the manna supply the people with the strength they needed to survive the rigors of the wilderness. (See Exodus 16:4, 19–20.)

Just as God instructed the Israelites to gather manna for their daily nourishment and strength, He too instructs us to feed daily on His Word. We all make excuses for not spending adequate time with God. But if we believe that God is our sole provider of time and energy, and that He gives us the wisdom to use those resources, then we shouldn't treat spending time with Him as a "job."

Psalm 119:97–104 reaffirms our need to spend time in the Word. The psalmist says, "Oh, how I love your law! I meditate on it all day long. Your commands make me *wiser* than my enemies, for they are ever with me. I have *more insights* than all my teachers, for I meditate on your statutes. I have *more understanding* than the elders, for I obey your precepts. I have kept my feet from every evil path so that I might obey your word. I have not departed from your laws, for you yourself have taught me. How sweet are your words to my taste, sweeter than honey to my mouth! I *gain understanding* from your precepts; therefore I hate every wrong path" (NIV, emphasis added).

No other words can feed and restore more than God's Word. Investing as little as ten to fifteen minutes daily to feed on God's words and to drink in the joy of His presence will renew our hearts and minds. Also, making the effort to "obey His precepts and meditate on His statutes" gives us the foundation for understanding God and gaining wisdom for everyday living.

For those of you who find it nearly impossible to maintain a consistent quiet time, let me suggest that you place a couple of devotional books around your home and/or workplace.

God understands the full and oftentimes stress-filled days of young mothers. Catching a few minutes with a devotional while you nurse the baby, while the children nap, or before everyone else wakes up in the morning can help you get refueled and refreshed while on the go.

Whether you're doing the dishes or driving the car, use that time to talk with God. As you rock your baby you can speak words of blessing and petition on behalf of your child. Not only will your prayers communicate love to your child, but you will also be talking to the only One who can ultimately make a difference in your life.

I must emphasize once again, regardless of the situations you face, make sure you spend time with the Lord. Do the best you can in your circumstances, but realize the more consistent you are in spending time with God, the more effective you will be in all areas of life.

The Word of God will feed and refresh your soul and spirit. The Bible is filled with words of strength and comfort. Take full advantage of this resource. The following passages are some of my favorites (taken from the NIV):

> Take my yoke upon you and learn from me, for I am gentle and humble in heart, and you will find rest for your souls. (Matthew 11:29)
> The Lord is good, a refuge in times of trouble. He cares for those who trust in him. (Nahum 1:7)
> You have been a refuge for the poor, a refuge for the needy in his distress, a shelter from the storm and a shade from the heat. (Isaiah 25:4)
> There remains, then, a Sabbath-rest for the people of God; for anyone who enters God's rest also rests from his

own works, just as God did from his. (Hebrews 4:9–10)

In this world you will have trouble. But take heart! I have overcome the world. (John 16:33)

Let the peace of Christ rule in your hearts, since as members of one body you were called to peace. And be *thankful*. Let the word of Christ dwell in you richly as you teach and admonish one another with all wisdom, and as you sing psalms, hymns and spiritual songs with *gratitude* in your hearts to God. And whatever you do, whether in word or deed, do it all in the name of the Lord Jesus *giving thanks* to God the Father through him. (Colossians 3:15–17)

If any of you lacks wisdom, he should ask God, who gives generously to all without finding fault, and it will be given to him. But when he asks, he must believe and not doubt, because he who doubts is like a wave of the sea, blown and tossed by the wind. (James 1:5–6)

Humble yourselves, therefore, under God's mighty hand, that he may lift you up in due time. Cast all your anxiety on him because he cares for you. (1 Peter 5:6–7)

Refreshed Through a Friend

God may refresh us through the love and help of a friend. When the apostle Paul was awaiting his execution in Rome, he spoke affectionately of his friend Onesiphorus who had searched high and low for Paul, risking his life to find his friend and bring him encouragement. Paul pronounced a blessing on Onesiphorus' entire household because of the great love this man had demonstrated: "May the Lord show mercy to the household of Onesiphorus, because he often refreshed me and was not ashamed of my chains" (2 Timothy 1:16, NIV).

The words of instruction and encouragement given to the church through the writings of Paul near the end of his life were made possible because Paul had a friend and fellow laborer in Christ who encouraged and *refreshed* him.

As I was working on these pages, my friend Ginger called to talk for a moment. I had intended to let the answering machine catch my calls while I worked, but instinctively, I answered the phone. Chatting for a moment, I mentioned that I was very tired and sincerely needed the Lord to speak to my heart. At that moment Ginger said, "Let's pray, sister!"

My friend began to refresh me through her loving prayer. Her request for God's divine wisdom bathed my soul in love and concern. By the time our conversation ended, I felt as though she had given me a cool drink of fresh water. Christ had refreshed me, but He had used my friend Ginger to do it.

Be Refreshed, but Also Be a Refresher!

We are refreshed and refueled as we allow the Word of God to feed our hearts and minds, and as we allow our friends to give us their prayers, words of encouragement, and presence. Those people in your life that are "refreshers," whether family or friends, need also to be refreshed. Before this day is over make that phone call or send a card thanking those who have shown God's love to you.

It's easy to overlook those whom God uses to refresh us. There is a little framed card in Heidi's room that reads, "A daughter is a joy bringer, a heart warmer, a memory maker. A daughter is Love." Not only did I want Heidi to know that I love and appreciate her, I also wanted her to be aware of the impact she has on another person's life.

I gave Nathan a similar card that says, "Son, never forget for a single minute, you not only grew under my heart, but in it." Each of the children have a drawer full of cards that express how proud we are to be their parents. These cards have been given for the most part on days when they did not expect it.

So often we demand help from our husbands and expect them to be there for us, but we must also look for opportunities to refresh *them*. That refreshment may come in the form of a card or love letter. It may come as a favorite meal, an affectionate hug, or an unexpected night of romance where you've arranged for the children to spend the night away and the two of you use the time to reconnect physically as well as spiritually and emotionally.

During one of our marriage seminars we asked couples to share some ideas of how they "refresh" each other. Here are a few of those ideas. Perhaps there's one you can use.

A man from International Falls, Minnesota, said, "I warmed up her side of the bed, and when she came to bed I scooted over." This may not mean much if you live in Miami, Florida, but in the "Refrigerator" of America, this is a supreme sacrifice.

One woman said, "I put a love note between two slices of bread in his lunch. Funny thing, though, he never mentioned it." She went on to say, "Since he never mentioned it, I decided not to mention it, either."

If you're going to do something refreshing for your spouse, make sure you exercise some caution. A woman told us, "I called his number at work, and before he could even say 'hello,' I said things to him that I knew would stir up anticipation for him coming home that evening. I was devastated when the female voice on the other end of the line said, 'I'll relay this message to Mr. Stinson.' "

Whether it's breakfast in bed (honestly, Steve doesn't like breakfast in bed—I guess it's the crumbs in the sheets), or taking out the trash without being asked, refreshing comes in the form of serving one another.

On my kitchen wall hangs a little poem Steve wrote years ago. It says:

> We believe a man and wife
> Would have a better married life
> If they would try out-serving one another.
> For deeper love is felt when what is done
> Is not for self
> But when it's done to satisfy the other.

For more suggestions on how to "out-serve" one another, read the chapter "Romance Starts With a Servant's Heart," in our book *Married Lovers, Married Friends* (Bethany House Publishers, 1989).

Smile at the Future

It was a rainy day in late October. With a shovel in one hand and a bucket of tulip bulbs in the other, I started to dig in my front yard. Carefully placing each bulb in the damp, cool ground, I knew it would be months before anyone would see evidence of my labor. Nevertheless, with my eye fixed on the future, I braved the cold, dank weather and planted the bulbs. As my hands became soiled and my jacket dampened, I continued on, looking forward to the pleasure of flowers in the springtime.

Proverbs 31:25 says of the virtuous woman, "Strength and

dignity are her clothing, and she smiles at the future." For generations, brave women have labored over flower beds, baby cribs, homework, and housework with the full knowledge that the work done now, though sometimes overlooked and quickly undone, will impact far beyond the present effort.

Courageous women, keep digging, planting, watering, and weeding. The beautiful harvest of our labor will yield a lasting fragrance in the lives of those we love.

"Let us not become weary in doing good, for at the proper time we will reap a harvest if we do not give up. Therefore, as we have opportunity, let us do good to all people . . ." (Galatians 6:9–10, NIV).

Finally, what do you do if you run out of fuel because you've let the needle drop below "E"? You do what I've done before: You get out and start walking!

In 1975, during a particularly difficult time in our lives, Steve wrote the following lyrics. Perhaps these words will encourage you as you continue your journey. God's speed—and see you at the finish line.

Keep on Walking[1]

Are you weary in well-doing,
    walking on the road to New Jerusalem?
Are you hoping and praying,
    looking any minute for the Lord to come?
And do you see a lot of pleasant-looking places,
    where you might lay down and take a rest.
If you do, take a look at all the faces there,
    their sadness will tell you that it's best to

Keep on walking; you don't know how far you've come;
Keep on walking; for all you know it may be done,
And the Father might be standing up
    right now to give the call
To call us home; keep on walking.

And if you need a feeling to keep you
    on that road you started traveling on,
You're going to have a problem,
    learning that it's faith that will keep you moving on,

---

[1]Words and music by Steve Chapman, as recorded on *For Times Like These* CD (Monk and Tid Music, SESAC, 1975). Used by permission.

'Cause, in the Lord, there's no time for sitting,
But sometimes, you have to take a stand;
Standing's not another word for "quitting";
It's just taking a tighter hold on His hand.

So keep on walking; you don't know how far you've come;
Keep on walking; for all you know it may be done,
And the Father might be standing up
    right now to give the call
To call us home. So keep on walking.

Acknowledgments

Good friends are hard to find, and in this maddening pace of life, they are even harder to keep. In my life, I am blessed to have three special friends. Not only do we share a great passion for the same issues (all of us dedicated pro-life and pro-family advocates), but we also share the same genetic pool. My sisters: Alice Click, Becky DeCoy, and Gayle Atwell add an appreciated quality and perspective to my life. Thanks, girls!

A special thank-you to Susan Andrews, who although great with child (welcome, Patrick) spent untold hours serving as sounding board, research assistant, and grammar editor during the writing of this book.

To my friends who have allowed their stories and thoughts to be used in these chapters, a hearty thank-you. Your willingness to share your life is a blessing to many.

Steve, Nathan, and Heidi, a thousand *thank-you*'s and *I-love-you*'s for enduring the writing process.